NOW
IS THE TIME
TO LOVE

John M. Drescher

Wipf and Stock Publishers
EUGENE, OREGON

Wipf and Stock Publishers
199 West 8th Avenue, Suite 3
Eugene, Oregon 97401

Now Is the Time to Love
By Drescher, John M.
©1970 Herald Press
ISBN: 1-57910-561-0
Publication date: January, 2001
Previously published by Herald Press, 1970.

DEDICATION

To Betty, my wife,
who helped make these pages possible,
and to our children,
John, Sandra, Rose, Joseph, and David,
who know best my failures to fully reach
the goals shared here
and also my deep desire to realize them
more completely.

Contents

Preface

Probably no part of society is more hungry for help today than young parents. This book was prepared with such in mind. Amid all the pessimism present regarding the family, these chapters seek to portray hope and the possibility of real happiness for any home.

Being a happy Christian family is not easy. There are no quick panaceas or plans. Pressures are great. But there is also much encouragement. The family, the first institution created by God, is not without His help.

Did you ever study the story of Noah recorded in Genesis? Great inspiration for each family can be found here. During days of the greatest moral decay ever recorded, Noah instilled in his children a respect for the moral law of God. At a time when every other family on earth turned its back on God, Noah's family faith was firm, so firm and strong that his children stood true in the face of ridicule and rabid rebellion against God and all that was good.

One can imagine Noah's children saying many things: "But Dad, no one else does it. Everyone else does this. We are the only family who lives like this. Why must we?" In contrast to the situation today, where most of us are surrounded with at least some others who love God, what these children said was literally true.

Noah's family alone loved and worshiped God. His family alone paid attention to God's commands. Noah placed God and His worship first in his home.

Through his firm faith and calm, confident commitment to God, Noah convinced his family and saw the salvation of all of them.

What a challenge! How could Noah do it? Was there

ever, before or since, such an example of what a God-honoring family is, what it can withstand, and what it is able to accomplish? And all this was under the law. What are the possibilities under grace and the power of the Holy Spirit!

This story in Scripture is certainly for our encouragement. If Noah could raise a family for God in the lowest period of history, may we be strengthened to see that by God's help we are not in a losing battle.

These chapters are the result of many things: much reading; courses taught in family conferences, camps, and congregations; counseling with families; and sharing in discussions with parents in small and large groups.

Because these thoughts, ideas, and illustrations were gathered over a period of time and from so many sources, it is difficult to give all the credit to the many who should receive credit. Credit is given wherever possible.

Several chapters grew out of writing assignments. Some of these chapters were printed in articles in different denominational magazines. One chapter was printed in more than two dozen different magazines.

These chapters are also an effort to capture in capsule form illustrations and insights which seemed to meet needs in numerous husband-wife and parent-child discussions. Since they opened opportunities for group sharing it is hoped that these chapters, now in book form, will furnish a basis for many more such discussions. For this reason several questions are introduced at the close of each chapter. A number of resource books are also listed at the conclusion of the book.

For best results it is suggested that no more than five couples be involved in one discussion group. When the group is larger some fear to participate. Others do not get a chance to share.

Now this small volume goes forth with the prayer that the goals shared here may be the means of blessing and encouragement to many homes for the glory of God and the good of each parent who may glean something herein.

1

Now Is the Time to Love

DADDY, I want to be with you." This statement from my three-year-old son was said three times before I looked up. I had urged him to go to bed several times. Each time he simply said, "Daddy, I want to be with you." Then to get my attention he asked a dozen questions. When I stopped writing he asked, "Daddy, why did you stop writing?" or "What are you thinking about now, Daddy?" When I started to write he asked, "What are you writing, Daddy?"

Finally, when he saw my real thoughts ignored him and that I was somewhat annoyed by his interruptions he slowly climbed down from his stool beside me and said quietly, "Daddy, I guess I'll go to bed now."

Then it hit me. My son was saying in his own way: "Won't you take time for me, Daddy? Please, Daddy, talk to me."

Just as he rounded the corner to the stairs I called after him, "Joey, come, let Daddy hold you before you go to bed. I want to talk to my boy a little while."

With a broad smile he came. I lifted him up and held him close. Then as he pattered off to bed a few minutes later I wondered how often my busyness caused me to miss golden opportunities to share my love with my children. I remembered those recurring statements I heard as a pastor, as a parent, as an instructor in family conferences and classes, and as I visited in many homes. They are statements such as these: "If only I had taken more time to enjoy my children." "If I had my family over again I would certainly take more time with them."

13

"Take time for your children now. They are soon gone."

Tomorrow Is Too Late

Now is the time to love. Tomorrow is too late to rock the baby. Tomorrow the toddler won't be asking questions. Tomorrow the schoolboy will not need help with his lessons. Nor will he bring home his school and neighborhood friends to share in family fun. Tomorrow the teenager will have made his major decisions and will not feel a need for the nearness he longs for and which we can give him now. And tomorrow our child will be close to us or a stranger to us depending upon how we use our time for him now.

Life lays the responsibility to take time to love upon parents at the very time when they bear the burdens of beginning a family and home. Father is struggling to get started in his lifework. Mother is busy feeding hungry faces, washing clothes, and cleaning house. At this time the call comes to love. At this time children need the warmth of parental love for personal well-being.

When children are small no other one thing or the abundance of things can take the place of love, which means to a large extent, taking time to be with our children, to answer their questions, to do things together, and to share the real meaning of life. Creating an atmosphere of caring and love in the home is the first step in teaching our children what love is and how to share love. To do this takes time.

But how do we take time? Without a doubt it is more difficult today than it was in the slow pace of past centuries. It is also the more necessary in light of the pursuits and pressures of our present day. Following are a few suggestions which may serve as a start.

Seek More Simplicity

Seek for more simplicity in living. We must guard against allowing the common concerns and activities of home, community, and even church life to rob us of the things most needful. A friend of mine turns the poem, by Joy Allison, "Which Loved Her Best," on parents and writes it this way:

> "I love you, Johnny," said Mother one day.
> "I love you more than I can say."
>
> Then she answered his questions with,
>   "Don't bother me now";
> And just didn't have time to show him how
> To tie his truck to his tractor and plow.
> But she washed her windows and scrubbed the floor
> And baked and cooked and cleaned some more.
>
> "Bring the neighbor in? Well, I should say not.
> You'll track up my floors and I don't want a spot.
> No, we won't have time for a story today.
> Mother's cooking for company, so run out and play.
> Maybe tomorrow," she said with a sigh,
> And Johnny went out almost ready to cry.
>
> "I love you, Johnny," again she said
> As she washed his face and sent him to bed.
> Now how do you think that Johnny guessed
> Whether 'twas he or the house that she really loved best?*

Today is known as a day of depersonalization. It can begin in the home itself where persons should care most for persons. And it often begins here when parents substitute things for themselves. We provide comfortable

* "I Love You, Johnny," written by a friend, Mary Klassen, is used with her permission.

and convenient homes. We give money for little extras. We may flood children with toys, sports equipment, clothes, books, and everything we as children longed for but did not have. Our giving to our children an abundance of things can easily be feeding our own need of security which our society says is in things. And things can become a substitute for personal involvement with our children. But unless we give ourselves and help them to give themselves all the things we may give them are of little worth.

Even in the abundance of things many children feel unloved. There are numerous cases of children whom we refer to as "having everything." Yet they hate their parents. Why?

One young man tells how his parents gave him a generous allowance, purchased whatever he desired, and loaded him with all kinds of presents, not only on his birthday and Christmas, but all through the year. The time came, when, in his inner anger, he threw the money in their faces and went through the house breaking his toys, because, as he said, it seemed to him his parents continually bought him off so that they would not need to spend time with him.

Love grows only as we give ourselves. Children do not need things nearly as much as they need love of parents. Yet one of the most common deceptions of today is that mother must go out to work to earn more money to buy more things "because she loves her children." Father feels he must moonlight to make more money to buy more things and bigger things because he "loves his family."

Because of this many children come almost daily to an empty house—one of the things which instills insecurity and resentment. They suffer also the tension and strain of tired nerves and bodies of both father and mother. And by a constant, consuming passion for things, on the part of parents, children are many times deprived of the very thing they need most—our love and ourselves. We buy things to show our love but don't have time to do things which demonstrate our love in the language children know.

Giving ourselves is not easy. Therefore, it takes purpose and planning. Someone has written, "Of course it is much easier to give things instead of ourselves just as it is easier to send a card than to pay an unhurried visit."

One father, after his son was beyond the time of persuasion and punishment, said, "I planned to go out with my boy and be his companion, when I had time. I resolved to attend church services regularly and to take him with me, when I had time. I hoped to interest him in young people's activities, when I had time. I promised I would talk to him like a father should to his son, when I had time. But for over twenty years for every one thought of my son I had a hundred thoughts of my business."

As one wise parent put it, "Do not pity the child who does not have a bicycle or whose parents cannot afford an encyclopedia. Pity the child whose parents do not have time to live with him, to teach him, to play with him, to express their love for him in many, many ways. The child without the bicycle and other material possessions, but with the warmth of parental love, is far happier than the poor rich child who has everything money can buy but lacks the needed security which comes through being loved 'in deed and in truth.' "

Some time ago a judge shared the answers he received from a young lawbreaker when he reminded him of his fine respected father, "I've often heard my father was a fine man," said the young man. "But I never knew him. He didn't have time for me."

Maybe if we stopped sometimes to consider we

would see that some of the things we stress such as spotless floors, accumulating of material things, and the rat race of social activities aren't nearly as important as we thought. King Solomon wisely said, "Better is a dinner of herbs where love is than a fatted ox and hatred with it" (Proverbs 15:17).

Make Time for Recreation

Seek to make time of recreation and leisure more family-centered. The family creates the atmosphere for receiving and giving love. Think back a moment. Are not the most meaningful experiences you remember in your childhood home those which you did as a family? Somehow these linger.

The other evening I visited a friend. I found him, with his family, in the backyard. They were sharing in a simple family barbecue. Such activities characterize his family and have built a great togetherness over the years.

Our family does some family camping. It is far less expensive than many types of recreation. And few kinds of recreation involve the whole family more than getting ready for a trip, packing, unpacking, setting up the tent, and getting meals ready. It is a money saver also in traveling. Dad and the boys take care of the tent. Mother and the girls share in selecting and cooking the food. And then there is the jolly, never-to-be-forgotten time, of climbing into sleeping bags, telling bedtime stories, and spending the night nestled together on a soft bed of pine needles.

If a family takes the time to plan occasions together it is surprising how many things can be done. I shall never forget the trip our family took to the zoo. So also a day at the art gallery or a trip to some historical landmark can be family-centered. Each family finds enjoyment in certain things and so each family needs to choose the kind of recreation the members enjoy. The important thing is that families do things together. For such times of planning and playing have great rewards and long remembrance. They help weave the tapestry of life into a beautiful pattern.

One mother shared the following: "From my own childhood I shall never forget the excitement and pleasure each summer as our whole family prepared for a one-day fishing trip not very far from home. There were seven children in the family. We would climb into the back of the old truck to go for a day of fishing, boating, swimming, walking on a swinging bridge, and eating a picnic lunch together. This was one thing, along with such spontaneous occasions as an all-family moonlight sledding party, which knit our home together in love."

Build Comradeship

Seek to build a spirit of comradeship. Love is built on relationships. The whole social and economic trend of today tends to pull families apart. This means that we must watch and plan for opportunities when we can work and play together. Our families need a spirit of comradeship. Some families set aside one night a week which is called home night. This takes top priority on all schedules.

Even when some members of the family need to be gone from home, a strong comradeship can still be built. It is built by the way those who are together remember the absent member.

"When I am gone from home," said one father, "I know that my family is thinking of me and praying for me. They know I am thinking of them and praying for them." Love and comradeship are not something we do or share only when we are together. Love is a way of life. It develops the "we" feeling.

Children not only long to belong but they easily develop the "we" feeling. Unless, for some reason, children are conditioned to the contrary, their arms and hearts are big. Their love reaches out. It is natural for children to love to do things together—whether in playing games, going for a walk, or planning a party. So it is natural for children to build a spirit of togetherness if it is encouraged by the parents.

Togetherness is encouraged by the parents when they allow their children to participate in family life. Many times parents stifle the spirit of togetherness or the feeling of belonging by impatience. When the small child wants to help his parents in little chores around the house he is sometimes shoved aside, told he is too small and to wait until he is bigger. While certain things must certainly be reserved for more maturity, yet participation in work, worship, play, and conversation is the creator of togetherness, comradeship, and belonging.

Perhaps parents too often take for granted that their children feel they belong and are loved. If we are asked as parents whether our children feel loved we'll immediately answer, "Why of course they are loved; we love all our children." Yet as someone said, "This is not enough. It is not how we feel but how they feel."

Many things create the feeling of "being loved." What are some of them? Children feel loved by the tone of our voice, by the way we hold them close, by the notice we give to their hurts and how we kiss their small injuries away, by the readiness to play with them and join in their laughter, by the time we take with them at bedtime in reading stories and hearing those last questions which linger in their minds, and by the little things which we allow them to do to help in our work. All these and many more such small things tell the tale of love. And now is the time to love in these many small ways.

Further, comradeship and participation are good preventives for discipline problems. One mother wrote about her experience in meeting the need of her adolescent daughter who became resentful and defiant. "Instead of punishing Betty and constantly reminding her of her age, I determined to give her large helpings of love and approval. I stopped ordering her to do certain expected duties, and asked her instead to work with me and share my duties. She previously had to do the evening dishes alone—which she did rebelliously—now we did them together, chattering as we worked.

"I made it a point to give her an affectionate hug now and then, and to praise her warmly when she deserved it. Both my husband and I laid aside our hobbies in the evenings to play games with her. . . . We gradually found our child again.

"We all love our children," says this mother, "but we forget to show them how much: by sharing with them our time, our hobbies, our work; by listening to them and giving them patient counsel or, if need be, intelligent and just punishment. That extra helping of love will enable our children to become mature and happy—as we want them to be."

Dorothy Baruch, psychologist and consultant in child guidance problems, points out in her book, *New Ways in Discipline,* that even the time we spend with our children may be the wrong kind. It is so often supervisory time, with focus on what the child should do, rather than on the child himself. This does not give a feeling of belonging or togetherness. Our time is on *things* and not on *him.*

Set-Times to Talk Together

Set aside definite times to just talk. It may sound strange to say that families should talk together. Yet the truth is that many families who stay in the same house live worlds apart. Close proximity does not prove that communication is carried on. Neither does living in the same house guarantee that families take time to talk together or that one knows what the other really thinks. Yet it is true that the warmth of our love as parents and children can be calculated to a great degree by how we talk and listen to each other.

Once a day at our house we plan for what we call family time. Some might call it family worship. But we do more than read the Bible and pray together as a family. It is also a time to talk together about many things. We cannot afford to do without this time together.

I like the suggestion of one author who says that maybe our mealtimes can be made more meaningful. She points out that dramatists stage family meals with frequent effectiveness. The novelist uses the talk around the table as a device to delineate character and for the promotion of a plot. One example this writer gives is Oliver Wendell Holmes who built his sage observations around the framework of the breakfast table.

As friends go out to eat together to discuss common concerns, so the family can use mealtime to discuss kindred concerns and build love and interest in one another. Love cannot really develop without shared experiences. Therefore, our families must find those times in which we can freely share our joys and sorrows, our delights and disappointments.

Because it is difficult to find time to do what we should does not mean that we should give up or fail to keep goals before us. One parent put it this way: "We may sometimes think that time with our youngsters is as illusive as the butterfly our little girl tries to catch. She reaches out for the desired object, only to have it elude her eager fingers. But this doesn't spoil her enjoyment in trying.

"Just so, we busy parents can enjoy trying. We, like she, will sometimes surprise ourselves and 'catch our butterfly.' "

NOW IS THE TIME TO LOVE

1. Is it true that the things you remember most clearly from your childhood are those things you did together as a family? What were some of these things?

2. What about priorities? Are too many activities, which in themselves may be good, taking you away from your family?

3. Discuss the whole subject of substituting things for ourselves.

4. How can your home do a better job of building a feeling of belonging on the part of your children?

2

When There's Love at Home

OUR marriage was about to break up," wrote a woman some time ago. "I didn't love John. Then I began to ask, 'How would I act if I did love my husband?' I consciously began learning his likes and dislikes. I prepared his favorite dishes. I joined in his hobbies. I bought surprises to put in his lunch. Now I love him with all my heart.

"But my greatest reward came the other day when our teenager said, 'Mom, I'm lucky!' 'Oh,' I answered, 'Why?' 'Because you and Dad love each other. You'd be surprised how many kids have parents who fight and quarrel most of the time.' "

Marriage is planned by God to be the interlocking of two lives in love for life. The wedding ceremony proclaims what God has produced through love. And there is no end to the possibilities of love.

Love, though much discussed, is difficult to define. There is a real sense in which only "love comprehendeth love." Further, there is much mix-up between "reel" love, which is a sorry mixture of selfishness and impurity covered over with a thick layer of purple passion, and real love, which does not bargain for itself but only begs to bless the other.

True love is more a matter of the will than of the emotion. Therefore, the Scripture can command us to love. God can say, "Husbands, love your wives. Wives, respect your husbands." The person who says he can no longer love is really confessing he lacks the will to love. Also "love is often the fruit of marriage," in the words of Moliere, as much as the root of marriage. One who spoke from a lifetime of family love said, "Love is what you've been through with somebody."

Without a doubt love is best defined by what it does. When we first fell in love there wasn't anything we weren't willing to do for the one we loved. We would go out of our way to see the other, do anything which we thought might please, and give little gifts to add to the other's joy. Remember that? Somehow we knew love cannot be passive. It is not love until it does something. And interestingly enough, the more we did, the more we loved. Love grows only as it is put into action.

Love Needs Nurture

Many marriage partners ought to learn all over again the practice of doing nice things for each other, without any reason or fanfare. Just do something out of love with no thought of return and see what happens.

You see, love must be cultivated to grow and this is a delicate process. It is nourished on the milk of human kindness. It flourishes on the common courtesies of thoughtful care. It ripens with mutual respect and reverence. Love cannot coast on past momentum. Without constant cultivation and nourishment it dies. In fact, if love does not mature it will prove insufficient. And maturing love is simply faithfulness in carrying out the daily duties and delights promoted by concern for another.

Thus we should not expect love to remain the same. The love of the teens is different from the love of the twenties. And the love of the twenties is different from the love of the thirties. Love has the longing within itself to grow larger and more beautiful.

A major part in maturing love is what might be called the "give and take" of love. Most of us realize it takes effort to "give" love. Too few make real effort to "take" love.

Bernie Wiebe, in a pamphlet on family living entitled *When Opinions Differ,* wrote, "Think about it a minute. How do you ordinarily receive a compliment? Someone says to you: 'That's a lovely dress you're wearing.' How do you answer? Do you say: 'Oh, it's just something I made in a hurry'? If that is your kind of reply, you actually don't allow yourself to 'take' that person's compliment. And you don't allow the giver the pleasure of giving. Or, have you learned to sincerely say 'thank you' or something like it, and really mean it?"

If love is best defined by what it does, then look at love's actions.

Love Is Kind

"Love is . . . kind," says the Scripture. "Be ye kind one to another, tenderhearted, forgiving one another, even as God for Christ's sake hath forgiven you. . . . And walk in love . . . as dear children." The advice is: "Live in love." How? By being kind, tender, and forgiving to others. And nowhere does this have greater claim or meaning than in the home.

Kindness is love in little things. And the small things of life make life gray or glorious because life is largely made up of little things.

As family members it is all too easy to develop an unkind disposition. We don't mean to but often the ones we love most bear the brunt of our discourtesy and irritability.

One mother had developed the habit of being cross and complaining. Away from her family she was all sweetness and light. One night after she was especially irritable, she heard her small child pray, "Dear God, make Mommy love me like she does the people we visit."

At first she thought the prayer was funny. She told it to her husband. He looked at her with a serious expression. Then he said, "You do not treat us with the courtesy you show to business people and our friends." It was a turning point for this mother. An old Scottish proverb says, "Remember, if you are not very kind, you are not very spiritual."

If the small considerations, courtesies, and kindnesses were essential in winning love in courtship these are just as essential in maintaining love in marriage. The ardor and attention and thoughtfulness of courtship dare not be allowed to turn to a look-out-for-yourself attitude in marriage. Sometimes one feels he can almost determine how many years certain couples have been married by the span between the trudging wife and her hurried husband.

We may have spotless and efficient households but without love and the warmth of affection our homes are like damp, dark, and cold castles of stone which produce only a deep desire to get away from it all.

Kindness, love in little things, on the other hand, adds warmth on the coldest night and gives us the desire to draw a little closer. While we wait for something big to happen, in which we might show our character, the truth is that Christian character comes forth the clearest in how faithful and loving we are in little things. And every happy home is made such by little acts and words of kindness.

Remember, courtesy and kindness are no more out-of-date than eating and sleeping. And these are just as necessary for the life of love as food and rest are for life itself.

Recently a friend of mine and a bride of nearly a year wrote: "I never before realized the importance of kindness, compliments, smiles, forgiving spirits, and voluntary helpfulness. It all ties together to make a good husband-and-wife relationship."

Frederick William Faber wrote: "Kind words are the music of the world. They have the power which seems to be beyond natural causes, as if they were some angels' song which had lost its way and came on earth. It seems as if they could almost do what in reality God alone can do—soften the hard and angry hearts of men. No one was ever corrected by a sarcasm—crushed, perhaps, if the sarcasm was clever enough, but drawn to God, never."

So the small words, "Please," "I'm sorry," "Excuse me," and "Let me help you," are love's words used in the ministry of kindness which may be achieved by all. And while great brilliance and intellect are to be admired, they cannot dry one tear or mend a broken spirit. Only kindness can accomplish this.

Love Needs Telling

For home happiness we must speak our love. Most marriage partners are too modest in expressing words of love. We seem to follow a fallacious old proverb or feeling which is expressed like this: "If we must tell another of our love, we really do not love." While there is a certain kind of truth told in this it is far from adequate.

All too often we are like the old Vermonter who sat on his porch whittling while his wife sat beside him rocking and knitting. After a long, long silence, the old man said, "You know, Sarah, you have meant so much to me that sometimes it's almost more 'an I can stand not to tell you about it."

An unknown writer put it this way:

"He never says, 'I love you so,'
As I somehow thought he would,
And if I ask, he says, 'You know
I do, that's understood.'

"For better or for worse,
The kind old parson chanted.
I don't know what John took me for,
But I took him for granted."

Love Is Long-suffering

Christian love loves in spite of faults and failings. This is a special character of Christian love. Christ loves us in spite of who we are and what we have done. And the Scripture says we are to love as He loves. "Love suffers long." That is, love bears up under the unpleasant and accepts others for what they are. Love, when it is true and pure love, does not burn with a zeal to change other persons. It just loves them. As Evan H. Hopkins says, "While faith makes all things possible, it is love that makes all things easy."

No one is free from faults. And in the home, where we are so familiar with our failures, this becomes most apparent. We may, if we wish, fix our attention on the faults of another, or we may choose to think on the good.

It is possible for a wife to see her husband's few faults and forget his many good points. She may find fault with her husband for hanging his clothes on the doorknob (and that is hard on a tidy wife) and fail to consider how good and kind her husband is, what a good provider he is, and how he helps with the many small chores around the house.

Then there is the husband who complains about the cooking (and someone said, "Burnt offerings are hard on a hearty eater"). But all the time he may forget he has a faithful and true wife, that her caring spirit and willing hands are always busy for another's good.

Yes, we all have faults. We decide whether we will think on the fine things or the faults in the lives of those dearest to us. It is good to learn to harp on the good things and let love cover a multitude of other things.

"Love is that which enables a woman to sing while she mops up the floor after her husband has walked across it in his barn boots," says the *Hoosier Farmer*. One might also add that love tells such a husband to cheerfully take off his boots next time.

Remember, love goes to the lovable. Said St. Thomas Aquinas, "To love anyone is nothing else than to wish that person good." Finally, the happiest mate is not the one who married the best person but the one who made the best of the one he married.

Love Can Laugh

Love has a sense of humor. We can't really be free to love if we take ourselves too seriously. We will be hurt at every turn. Love develops the funny bone rather than the tear ducts.

A recent writer tells of a husband who put a coin in a machine which turned out a ticket telling his fortune and weight. He read statements like, "You are a fine person whom all the opposite sex admire and follow after." His wife, who had a keen sense of humor, glanced over his shoulder, read the statement with a smile, and said, "I notice, dear, that they have your weight wrong also."

Remember, true love allows one to laugh as long as it does not belittle a lover and as long as it laughs with another and not at another.

Finally, in the words of Hazen G. Werner: "Family love and understanding are made complete when God is there; the lives of all members of the family depend on the ultimate good, life with God."

This brings us to the key of the Christian home. We who claim to be children of God can expect that God will impart that special divine love to us His children. A selfish heart cannot love unselfishly. But He promises a new heart. We now offer ourselves as channels for His love to flow through to our family and to others. Whenever this happens, our homes will experience a holy and heavenly affection.

WHEN THERE'S LOVE AT HOME

1. What do you think of the idea that true love is more a matter of the will than of the emotion? Is it true that when one says, "I can no longer love that person," he really is saying, "I no longer want to love him"?

2. List ways of nurturing love in marriage.

3. Why are we hesitant to tell our love? Is it true that we feel the need to be told that we are loved but that we feel the other person has no such need?

4. What is the place of humor in a happy family? Each one share something humorous you remember from your family's experience.

3

Communicate or Burst

A large class of husbands and wives met several nights a week for a period of six weeks to study, in a rather intimate way, family relationships. In the first session I suggested that each person answer two questions: What is the primary problem in your marriage? What do you plan to do about it?

Each person was asked to write answers to these questions and submit the response to me at the close of the course. Each felt free to submit answers since no name needed to be attached.

Responses were good. And the responses revealed what many marriage counselors say is a primary problem in marriage: a problem of communication.

Papers came to me with such statements as: "Our biggest problem is that we can't really talk together." "We don't discuss our problems." "We never talk about things that really matter. It's all superficial talk." "Ours is a breakdown in communication. Either we remain stone silent when we face a problem or we blast off at each other." "I wish we could really talk things over together."

What Happens?

Although communication is basic in building confidence and love in courtship, it seems after marriage many times something happens. One writer puts it like this: "If you see a couple sitting in a restaurant, in the park, or anywhere in public, watch the conversation. If the woman is obviously impressed by each word the man murmurs, if he in turn eagerly awaits and welcomes her response, you can take it as a fact—unmarried.

"But if she gazes absently in one direction, he stares in another; when one's lips move, the other gives little or no indication of hearing, don't bother looking for a wedding ring. They couldn't be more married.

"Oh, yes, there are exceptions. Those few couples who cultivate the fine art of con munication. . . . Strange, isn't it that a couple falls 'n love by communication, nourishes it with their unique codes of communication, and unite in the spiritual, emotional, and physical communication of marriage--then suddenly they become speechless! Suddenly they can't or don't get through to each other anymore."

Perhaps part of the problem begins because each, in coming into marriage, has an idyllic picture of what marriage ought to be. Naturally, there is some clashing of these ideals. For fear of hurting or disturbing each other, or because an argument usually develops over differences, communication ceases. And since small problems or large problems, which every marriage faces, are not handled in an open and mature manner, lovers drift apart. The difference between happiness and unhappiness is not that one marriage has less problems or more problems than another marria ʒe but rather that one couple has learned the art of talkii g things over and the other has not. Harmony comes an(love is strengthened by a frank and honest discussion ‹ f differences.

In addition, studies indicate a clos(relationship between the parents' level of communication between themselves and the communication they experience between themselves and their children. The child-parent communication gap begins with a father-mother communication gap. When mother and father have learned to talk together fully, freely, and in love and openness;

when father and mother really listen to what the other is saying, children develop a free, open, and sharing spirit also.

Whenever parents notice they are curt to each other or that their children are fighty, fussy, and frustrated, it is time to stop and ask, "What's going on here?" Likely they'll find poor communication between themselves as husband and wife.

Dr. Paul Popenoe, founder and president of the American Institute of Family Relations, believes that the problem of the delinquent child can hardly be helped until something "is done to create a harmonious relationship between parents." So quarreling about children, the No. 1 source of husband-wife conflict, is not the result of parenthood problems, but of marital problems.

Communication the Core

One experienced counselor was asked: "What is the most essential characteristic of a happy marriage?" He replied, "After love, the ability to confide fully, freely, and frankly in each other." Another well-known marriage counselor found the failure to converse was a "frequent factor in middle-age conflicts and almost universal in all unhappy marriages." A study in an Eastern college states, "Nothing is more apt to smooth the course of love than communication; the level of marital satisfaction appeared to be related to the amount of time each day a couple spent talking together." Marriage is really a lifetime of relationships dependent upon communication.

What marriage counselor can forget the typical wife who comes to pour out her feelings about the actions and attitudes of her husband? Her husband is rude in relationships with her. He doesn't respect her feelings in making love. He hurries, is impatient, and ignores her feelings. If he loved her he would do differently. But when asked if she ever discussed this with her husband, she says, "No." The husband's story is similar. His wife is always tired, indifferent to his feelings, and frigid. If she really loved him she would be sensitive to his needs and know how he feels. But when asked if he ever discussed this with his wife his answer is also "No."

This example is one of many. The chief tool God gives us to understand each other is conversation. Many of the adjustments of marriage could be cleared up easily if faced frankly and discussed freely. Yet because we do not talk, small irritations become tremendous trifles.

Our Method of Escape

But communication at the deep levels of life is difficult. So we seek methods of escape. Urban G. Steinmetz, in his book, *I Will,* suggests many of the subtle things we do to avoid serious conversation. We may not always be aware of what we are doing. He calls such, "avoidance technologies." For instance, when we do not want to talk about our problems, we become busy at some project. Husband stays at the office day and night. Wife needs to scrub floors, wash dishes, pack lunches, and do many other evening jobs around the house.

Even going out with another couple for a good evening together can be an avoidance technique. It keeps husband and wife from talking by themselves. So magazines and books, hobbies, bridge clubs, bowling leagues, golfing, and a hundred other things are often escape routes so that husband and wife are not left alone together long enough to deal with differences or difficulties.

TV provides a primary escape today. A recent study of suburban Chicago says, "A typical suburban family is found huddling around a television screen listening to other people talk. But there is no talk among those watching. There is no feeling and sharing, and therefore, loneliness, isolation, and lack of love become the pattern of daily living."

Who has not used such escapes? For the more religious, Steinmetz says that many things, such as PTA, the Ladies' Auxiliary, the midweek church meeting, church committees, planning commissions, library boards, and many similar "good things," keep husband and wife occupied. Says Steinmetz, "Do-goodism is a very insidious way of avoiding necessary conversations. We all feel so good about it while we're doing it. Our son Jim had to remind us awhile back, 'What are you doing, going out again tonight to tell other people how to raise their kids? We'd like to talk to you, too, once in a while.' "

Communication Stoppers

All of us sometimes do simple things which stop the possibility for further communication after talking has begun. Some select silence as a weapon. And it's a cruel weapon. Phillis McGinley wrote:

> Sticks and stones are hard on bones
> Aimed with angry art,
> Words can sting like anything,
> But silence breaks the heart.

Sometimes silence is golden. The Scripture says, "There is . . . a time to keep silence, and a time to speak." But where problems exist the deep freeze of silence is seldom a solution. In marriage silence is dangerous because silence also speaks. Silence shouts that something is wrong. Love can survive large problems better in the open than small ones burning and smoldering within. Silence can make life difficult.

Ivy Moody tells of a visitor watching his old friend plow. "I don't want to butt in," he said, "but you could save yourself a lot of work by saying 'gee' and 'haw' to that mule instead of just tugging on the lines." The old-timer mopped his brow and agreed. "Yep, I know that, but this mule kicked me six years ago and I ain't spoken to him since."

Silence is really a lack of love. It implies the other is not worth sharing a concern with, that we don't care what the other thinks, and that the other will not contribute toward an understanding.

Some stop communication by words of sarcasm, ridicule, or making fun of the other. All these are forms of hostility. These hurt. So do the words "You never" or "You always." These ought never be used because they are barbs which harm and never help, plus the fact that they just are not true. Think about it a moment. It just is not true that we never do or always do a thing. Often these little phrases stop a conversation because a blanket statement such as this puts out any spark of hope for understanding and conversation.

Sometimes bringing up the past is a good stopper. One man in reporting on his wife, said, "When I began to talk, she became historical." "You mean hysterical," her friend said. "No," he said, "I mean historical. She brought up everything I ever did." Bringing up the past is a way to stop communication. If the past must be discussed, then discuss it to completion and forget it. Do it once and for all. Then forgive and forget.

Making the other feel cheap or ignorant is a communication stopper. Some wives stop communication by starting to cry. Some husbands slam doors and leave the room. Such conduct constitutes a childish, rather than a mature way of meeting issues. And every family must face problems sooner or later if happiness is to reign.

Marriage and Maturity

No position in life offers more chance for advancement and maturity than marriage. Yet here of all places we are most afraid to face ourselves. But if we are willing to face ourselves, there is no end to the possibilities for growth.

Who knows you better—your weaknesses and strengths—than the person you are married to? Who ought to be able to point these out to you better than the one you love and the one who loves you? Who is more interested in making you a better person than the one whose very life depends on you? So also, by using each other as sounding boards, you are able to test your thoughts, ideas, and plans. There is great blessing in learning how to complement one another.

If we are to help one another several things are needed. First we will need to really listen to what the other is saying. To communicate means to forget ourselves, to listen, to try to understand the other's point of view. The only kind of communication which can help is that which is willing to say, "I know I may not think or act like you but I will try to understand how you feel about this."

Marriage takes a special kind of communication—an empathetic "feeling with" the other. Listening includes trying to understand what people mean, as well as paying attention to their words. When a husband says, "I guess you are too tired to make love tonight," it is understanding that he wants the assurance from his wife that she is not too tired. Communication depends as much upon the quality of listening as upon the quality of speaking.

Too often we listen, not to learn, but only until we can find some mistake or think of something to fire back in defense of ourselves. And since we cannot see ourselves without another's help we not only lose insight which could make us better persons but we stop communication.

Second, real communication is based on a climate of confidence, trust, and love. To share inmost thoughts, feelings, and experience depends on the safety one feels in receiving and giving confidences and in the knowledge that what is shared will not be ridiculed or misunderstood. It persists in the persuasion that what is said will be taken seriously.

All enter marriage timid, bashful, and fearful of what the other might think if innermost thoughts and feelings are shared. Will love be lessened and will the bond of marriage be weakened if all is told? Only when there is a love which conveys a true spirit of acceptance and concern, regardless of what is said, can there be real communication.

Paul Tournier points out that when a husband complains, "But she doesn't understand me," or "I just can't understand that woman," he is really saying in shorthand, "I don't think she accepts me," or "I can't accept my wife." But the commitment to be understanding, loving, and accepting can begin to change that.

Next ingredient of good communication in marriage is the actual decision to share fully feelings, failings, and fears, as well as joys, pleasures, and wishes. Marriage dare make no room for reservations. Keep hearts open. Share thoughts freely. It means giving our own bodies completely and releasing our souls reverently to each other, until, as Erasman says, "The wedlock of minds will be greater than that of bodies."

True communication is self-disclosure, self-revelation. Masks must be dropped. Pretense must be put away. Defenses must fall. Guards must go. Finances, in-laws, sex feelings, child discipline—all these and more must be talked about. Marriages break, not because of talking, but because partners do not talk. It is those couples who are free to discuss fears and frustrations, as well as joys and delights at the deepest levels and without limits, who experience a growing closeness.

Complete the Argument

A word should be said yet about the danger of never really talking things through to the finish. Tensions build up in every home at times to the boiling point. We are bothered by each other and many everyday irritations. What should be done? We can boil within with bitterness until ulcers develop, or we can talk about it even though our voices get loud. It is good sometimes to hear our feelings put into words so that we can see how exaggerated they are and really discuss them. It is much more dangerous and damaging to discuss things half and then harbor hurt and hostile feelings inside than to say it like we think it is. Said one authority, "Divorces are caused by communications not completed." Halfway discussions have only harmful effects. Few marriages break because of big things but because of small irritations left undiscussed or unconfessed.

A striking statement in Scripture says, "Do not let the sun go down on your anger, and give no opportunity to the devil" (Ephesians 4:26). In other words never go to sleep with a sense of bitterness. Clear up every ill feeling or wrong before bedtime. There is an inner injury and illness when resentment remains. It can lead to the death of love. In addition, our physical and emotional life cannot bear the burden of bitterness without serious results. One leader challenged his listeners to think if they knew of any couple continually at odds who lived to celebrate their fiftieth-wedding anniversary. His point was that the toll bitterness takes in life is too great for our physical bodies to last long.

An unwillingness to discuss feelings and acts also allows the devil to do his work of division and destruction. So the Scripture says we are to settle things and give no "place to the devil."

Although discussion of deep and real problems which every home has is hard, it is still the best medicine to make a strong marriage. Bravery and honesty are needed to share innermost thoughts, even though it runs the risk of heated argument. This is far better than burning, buried bitterness.

Dr. Wendall Watters, Canadian psychiatrist, says that couples who avoid "hot negotiations" have coldly impersonal distant relationships. True love compels us to share not only the nice things but also the things which disturb. It is good to remember we didn't marry the perfect person we dreamed about. It's good to remember we are real persons with feet of clay who make plenty of mistakes. The husband and wife who say they never had an argument are either very good forgetters or never really learned to know each other as real persons. There are those husbands and wives who never really share the joy of knowing each other. They have a growing loneliness with the passing years.

Some time ago a speaker shared what he said was a sure formula for starting communication again if it had broken down. It is guaranteed, he said, if followed. Let husband and wife sit on chairs facing each other so close that knees touch. Let them hold hands and look into each other's eyes for fifteen minutes, no more, no less, without a word. How long has it been since you looked long into each other's eyes? In courtship you spent hours together. You used every opportunity to be together, to hold hands and look into each other's eyes. Now do it again.

One of the first things which will happen is that each will likely begin to laugh. Humor is a good communicator. Many times we take ourselves too seriously and bv so doing cut the lines of communication.

A friend told this story: Early in the marriage of Don and Mary they had pie for supper. It was the first piecrust Mary had made. Some days after the pie was served Mary found out that Don had on the sly slipped the crust to the dog. She was hurt deeply. When Don returned home she told him about it in no uncertain terms.

Don was quiet for a few moments, then said, "Mary, I was afraid for a while that even the dog wouldn't eat it." With that both burst into laughter and fell into each other's arms.

"At that moment," said Mary, "Don and I pledged we would discuss everything together. We promised to be open and frank with each other and not hide our feelings or thoughts ever again. And believe it or not, we are still friends after fifteen years."

COMMUNICATE OR BURST

1. Is communication a problem in your marriage? Examples?

2. What do you think of the statement that the generation communication gap begins with the mother-father communication gap?

3. Do you find in your experience that you engage in hobbies, busywork, and recreation to escape the hard task of really talking things through?

4. Do you feel you can be free to talk with your partner about your feelings, frustrations, and fears without losing confidence and love? Why?

4

Like Parent, Like Child

MOTHER, working in the kitchen, heard quarreling. The noise became louder and louder.

"Stop quarreling!" she said as she stepped into the living room. "You know that never settles anything. Quiet down and quit fussing at each other."

Imagine her surprise when one of the children replied, "But Mother, we aren't quarreling. We are only playing Daddy and Mother." Those parents didn't know what they were teaching.

From the earliest moments in life, the child is a "copycat." This is a way of learning. Copying covers every area of life. Play is patterned after the parents' actions. Children also imitate body posture, habits, tone of voice, diction, and vocabulary. Much baby talk is merely the result of adults talking baby talk. It is usually just as easy for a child to copy correct words as incorrect ones. Hohman writes in *As the Twig Is Bent,* "The most potent influence in child culture is imitation."

The atmosphere of the home cannot be touched. But it can be felt. It is a thing of the spirit. No photographic plate is as sensitive as the spirit of a child. The images which lodge there determine the direction and destiny of life. By numberless little things and unconscious influence, we weave our child's character, thread by thread. As surely as we provide our child's clothes and food, we, by our example, help form his habits and give him what will strengthen or weaken him for life.

Home Molds Child's Character

As our child grows, he carries in his character the subtle impressions of his home. If the atmosphere is one of love, he absorbs it. If the atmosphere is one of trust and fidelity, he goes forward trusting and to be trusted.

What creates the atmosphere of a home? Our attitudes toward one another and toward others help create it. The basic determining factors in our day-to-day living help determine the atmosphere in our homes and also are the essence of our faith. It is this which we pass on to our children.

By simple means we earn respect and love. If we have time for our children, we find that our children have time for us. If we express love and devotion by the way we speak to our children, by the way we hold them close, and even by the way we exchange smiles, we build love and devotion.

If we prove by our actions that we want our children today, our children will want us tomorrow. If we say kind things about them and express sincere concern for others, our children will learn to respect, love, and care for others. The opposite is also true. Our irritations are rubbed off on our children. Our gossip sets their "teeth on edge."

Many times the atmosphere of our homes is determined more by our reactions than by our actions. The calm response of one father to the cursing and accusations of an angry neighbor left an indelible impression upon a young man who today serves with confidence and calmness in a most difficult and critical position.

How do we react to catastrophe? Have you noticed how some children react when they fall out of a swing or get hurt while playing? Some jump up, brush off the dust, and go back to play without blaming anyone else. Others cry angrily, fix the blame on someone else, and run off to pout. We, as parents, by our reactions, often determine how our child responds in these situations. Our children react the way they see us react.

It's striking how the same father who says, "It's only the kid calling," finds later in life he has a son who says, "It's only the old man yakking." Its striking how the same mother who says, "I don't have time for a story tonight," finds later in life that she has a child who says, "I don't have time to visit Mom." It's striking how the same parent who calls his child a little rascal or devil finds that his child always lives up to his reputation.

On the other hand, it is just as striking how the same father who takes time to listen to his son finds a son anxious to hear his words. It's striking how a mother who counts time with her children precious has children whose thoughts and visits later in life often turn homeward. Striking, too that the parent whose thoughts and words indicate love toward his children finds love and trust returned. "With what measure ye mete, it shall be measured to you again." "Cast thy bread upon the waters: for thou shalt find it after many days." We can choose the judgment and the kind of bread we want returned.

Children Register Reactions

Emotional reactions attract children quickly. F. H. Richardson in *Parenthood and the Newer Psychology* writes, "We knew that (the child) . . . can and does unconsciously register parental tricks and habits and mannerisms at an age which seems impossible that he should be taking conscious note of his surroundings."

Attitudes are as contagious as whooping cough and much more lasting. Here is where we as parents most often give ourselves away. We can teach disrespect for the law by our attitudes. I know a father who deplores juvenile delinquency, yet disregards speed limits and stop signs. He brags in front of his children of the time he was caught speeding but cleverly escaped from paying a fine. Should such a father be surprised when his son is a lawbreaker in the home, school, or community?

Sometimes active church members cannot understand why their children do not seem interested in the church and its activities. But what kind of attitudes are rubbed off when parents complain about the amount of time the church claims, about the preacher's long sermons, and the choir's poor singing?

One father, on learning that his son stole several pencils from the department store, scolded him severely and said, "You ought to know better than to steal. I can pick up all the pencils you need at the office."

What lessons in honesty do our children learn when parents bring home pencils, stationery, tools, and other items belonging to employers? What can we expect to result from the devious business deal or sly income-tax deduction discussed over the dinner table? Is it surprising that in a recent survey many college students said that cheating is standard practice, and some saw nothing wrong, as long as one didn't get caught?

"The other evening," a Christian leader wrote, "I attended a Cub Scout meeting. The son of my friend was to be advanced a rank. One of the pledges exacted of the boy was that he should not smoke tobacco. No one in the group even smiled when the lad took the oath with upraised hand, and twelve mothers and fathers in the group smoked either cigarettes, cigars, or pipes."

I know a father who practices keeping his promises. No matter how small the child or the promise, he seeks to keep his promise. Confidence, honesty, and integrity are being built into his son. I also know a father who pushes his child off with promises, only to forget them. This father destroys the very structure of character which is hard to rebuild.

So, also, when we give our children a dollar for amusements and a dime for the church offering, we tell them that self-indulgence is ten times more important than Christian benevolence.

A small child carefully constructed a building of blocks. He was intensely interested in his project. Suddenly, it was time for bed. His father called him to come. It was time to put the blocks away—now! In spite of the cries or feelings of his child, with one sweep and without further explanation, he crumbled the child's creation.

Sometime later this chld, impulsively and seemingly without concern of conscience, destroyed a prized possession of his parents. Was there any resemblance to the father's action?

My small daughter and I were waiting our turn in the doctor's office. A family entered with two small boys. The smaller son would not allow his parents to remove his heavy jacket or cap out of fear of the doctor.

Soon, however, he was playing happily but too noisily for a doctor's office. To keep him from breaking the lamp, tearing the magazines, and annoying others, the parents tried to scare him into obedience a dozen times by telling him the doctor was coming, the bogeyman would get him, or that he would get a spanking when he got home. The little fellow, after a warning or two, paid no attention. Why should he? Such parents were teaching their child not only to fear a friend, but also to mistrust their own words.

Children usually live up to the reputation parents give them. Some time ago I was in a home where the parents were continually commenting concerning the awful behavior of their three-year-old. Time and again the parents said, "He's a bad one." "He's a little rascal," or "He doesn't know how to behave."

And the three-year-old demonstrated before us that he was doing all in his power to live up to his reputation. Think of the power positive comments could well have had.

Child Echoed Parents

Here are parents who find their son expelled from school because he spoke disrespectfully to a teacher. Not only did they find him unrepentant, but he rebelled against making any admission that he did wrong. The parents were horrified. However, they did not reflect on the times when they, in their son's presence, had spoken disparagingly of the school administrators and the school faculty.

Seemingly, they did not think they were teaching when they made such statements as, "Teaching used to be a respected profession. Today it's a job for misfits and those who can't do anything else."

As parents we are teachers without a holiday. Since the actions of our children which disturb us most are usually reflections of our performance, we should look honestly at ourselves. We must seek to be real persons

—void of hypocrisy. We must put more emphasis on being the right kind of examples.

"Do you mean," asked a father who was participating in a parents' discussion group, "that a parent should ever admit to his child that he has made a mistake?"

Certainly. Parents owe it to their children to admit their errors. The well-adjusted children do not necessarily come from the home where parents make the fewest mistakes. They likely come from a home where parents make many mistakes but are frank and honest enough to admit them.

Some think it is a sign of weakness to admit a mistake. The opposite is true. Admitting error when it is an error is a sign of strength and maturity. It is also the first step to improvement and the winning of respect.

By no amount of pretending perfection do we persuade our children that we are flawless. For a parent to admit a mistake is to instill respect for truth and the desire to do right. I sometimes think I can read the reactions of parents in the way children react. The fact is that our children learn how to react by the type of reactions we as parents demonstrate, particularly during times of tension and trying circumstances.

A time or two a week, during the summer months, I stop by the park to watch the Little League playing ball. The earnestness and spirit of these boys is most intriguing. Such seriousness and joy are hardly surpassed at any other age.

Of particular interest to me is the way the boys react when they commit an error, when they strike out, or when they are put out on base.

Did you ever notice that nearly every ball team has the "pebble finder"? He's the fellow who picks up some small pebble or clod and throws it from the spot when he commits an error. He pretends that a pebble made the ball bounce wrong or in some way interfered with his play.

Or take the example of the fellow I saw the other evening. The ball seemed to go right through his glove. He immediately began to check the leather lace in his glove, letting all know that his glove must certainly be at fault. Some boys rather consistently come in from an inning with the complaint that they were tripped or the umpire was wrong.

Then there is the other type of fellow. When he commits an error, he also takes it seriously. You can see it all over his face. But when he comes off the field I hear him say, "Man, I goofed on that one. I should have caught that ball easily." Or when he strikes out at the plate his characteristic comment is, not that the umpire was wrong, but—"That's the one I should have hit!"

We want our children to grow up to hold their own in a world where people will often be wrong. We want our children to stand up for what they know to be right. The desire to seek the truth, not merely to look for a way to save face, is what they need to learn from us as parents.

We must be alert to teaching opportunities in direct teaching situations. But more, since most of our teaching is by indirect teaching and since we are really teaching all the time whether we want to or not, we must be on guard, exercising self-control, and in constant dependence on divine help.

Years ago a mother wrote, "Do you ask what will educate your son? Your example will educate him; your conversation with your friends; the business he sees you transact; the likings and dislikings he sees you express —these will educate him. . . . Your . . . station in life, your home, your table will educate him. . . . Education goes on every instant of time; you neither stop it nor turn its course. What these have a tendency to make your child, that he will be all of his life."

LIKE PARENT,
LIKE CHILD

1. Discuss the fact that it seems some children from very good homes do not turn out good.

2. Did you ever notice that when you as a parent are irritable the children seem also to be fussy and irritable and when you are happy that children are happy also? Is this imaginary or real?

3. Give illustrations of children registering reactions of parents. Every home has some stories like this to tell.

4. In what way is it more or less difficult to raise well-adjusted, happy children today than years ago?

5

Making
Family Life Spiritual

BUT Daddy, we didn't pray." These words came from four-year-old Sandra in the back seat of the car.

I had decided, on the spur of the moment, to conduct an experiment. Instead of following our usual practice of bowing our heads for prayer previous to taking our trip, I started the car and began to back out of the driveway. Would any of the children notice the omission? I wondered. They did. It was voiced immediately by Sandra.

One of the greatest opportunities parents possess, yet one which is most easily passed by, is to make great moments of family life deeply spiritual in character.

Take this matter of family trips. We started to take just a moment, before starting on a trip, to pray for God's guidance and blessing on our travel. It seems like a simple thing, yet it is a meaningful opportunity to teach not only the importance of prayer in the ordinary things of life, but also it is a natural in leading our children to look to God for guidance and care.

So it is that many happenings and events of family life have great potential to instill spiritual insight and blessing. This does not mean that a prayer or sermon is inserted at every turn. Not at all. Rather, we should seize those opportunities in family living which can do much in building our lives and homes for God.

Look, for instance, at what the birth of a baby in the home can mean for the entire family. This is a great moment which can be made deeply spiritual in character. Each one in the family can share in the great miracle of life. To thank God together for a new member of the family and unitedly dedicate the child to God cannot help but leave an indelible spiritual impact upon the family.

"I know," said a young college girl, "that my family dedicated me to God before and after I was born. With each new brother or sister, I heard my parents pray prayers of dedication. I always knew each child in our family was looked upon as a blessing from God. God's blessing and guidance were daily prayed upon our lives."

When We Walk by the Way

Many times I am struck by the spontaneous expressions of a child concerning God's creation. At every turn a child can see God's handiwork. A stroll by some stream or through the park poses new opportunities of learning, both natural and spiritual. What parent can forget such questions as, "Daddy, how do the stars stay up in the sky? What makes some stones round and other stones sharp? and How did God make the mountains so high?" What better questions are ever asked to lead into conversation concerning God's greatness and glory?

What should parents do when the spontaneous questions and experiences of children lead to holy ground? Long ago Job was told "stand still, think of the wonders of God." Too often parents pass by these opportunities rather than taking time to ponder with their children the wonders of God.

A friend of mine expressed their family goal this way: "We try to catch moments of beauty whenever they come or wherever they are and relate them to God and His plan for the total universe. Many times the

children's concerns and interests lead to the threshold of
worship." She gives this example. "Fifth-grader Billy
brought home his *Weekly Reader* so that his mother
and daddy could 'learn about whales too.' Supper talk
was a mixture of football and whales. When supper was
over, Billy's dad read these words from the Bible: "And
God created great whales . . . and God saw that it was
good."

"You see, Billy," said his father, "even whales are a
part of God's great plan."

Blessed by Belonging

Few moments of family life are better for adding spiritual dimension than birthdays. Birthdays are milestones
in the mind of a child. They can also be spiritual milestones when the emphasis is on belonging and sharing,
and the feeling of belonging and sharing is not realized
by giving of gifts but by giving ourselves. Some children
have received large gifts and all the time felt hated.

Take the case of one child whose family provided a
large cake, an abundance of new clothes and toys, along
with a sizable gift of money for the occasion. But with
all the gifts, the child keenly felt neglected by his
parents. There was no sense of really belonging. As he
recalls, he "seemed to sense inside that his parents were
avoiding giving themselves by giving other things."

Another young man speaks about the way his family
celebrated his birthday when he was a child. Too poor
to purchase gifts, yet with the cake his mother made
and the candles kept from former birthdays, combined
with the love expressed, he had a deep sense of belonging. Further, by the way the family shared in making
this a great day and by the way the spoke about *their*
boy and brother growing older and taller gave him a
sense of worth and well-being. "I remember also," he

says, "the prayer my father prayed at the birthday meal. I knew my family and God in heaven were interested in me and I belonged to all of them." How easy it is for a child's understanding to move from belonging to such a family to belonging to God's family.

Pausing for prayer before starting for church Sunday morning makes churchgoing more than a routine or meaningless ritual. To pray for those who minister and teach and to ask God for a fresh insight of His will does not go unrewarded in building a love for God, His church, and His Word.

A beloved pastor, now in his nineties, had many ways of making moments in the home deeply spiritual in character. One example was the blessing he gave departing guests.

When a family left his doorstep, they always walked away with a fresh God-consciousness. His daughter, now a college professor, wrote words of gratitude when reflecting on her home experience. When family and friends paused before farewells, her father asked them to join in a Scripture, song, or prayer together. "Often," she said, "if the guests were traveling from a distance, we said the travelers' psalm or sang:

> As I journey through the land, singing as I go,
> Pointing souls to Calvary, to the crimson flow,
> Many arrows pierce my soul, from without, within,
> But my Lord leads me on, through Him I must win.
>
> Oh, I want to see Him, look upon His face,
> There to sing forever of His saving grace;
> On the streets of glory, let me lift my voice,
> Cares all past, home at last, ever to rejoice.

"The words of the song, 'elect from every nation, yet one o'er all the earth,' took on meaning as we prayed together in our Ohio parsonage with friends new and old from east, west, north, south, and lands abroad."

Our Fun and Our Faith

In a day of much family camping and travel how can our families make these experiences deeply spiritual? Such occasions afford some of the easiest opportunities to call attention to God's creation. One young man reflected on just such an experience and wrote: "Some of my highest spiritual moments have been at family devotions in family camping."

Who has not felt spiritually strengthened while standing under the starry sky or sitting by a campfire surrounded by God's handiwork?

One family took the Bible touring with them on vacation. When travel grew tiresome the mother reached for the Bible and turned to Psalm 121. "I will lift up mine eyes unto the hills," she read. Then the family repeated after her, "I will lift up mine eyes unto the hills."

Through Psalm 121 and the family repeating it, the children received an impression which caused ten-year-old Anne to remark, as they reached the majestic Rockies, "I'm glad we learned those verses about the hills, Mother, for today."

Some time ago two of our children came home from a school field trip and told us that the children on the bus sang nearly all the time they traveled. This was not new for our children, for we sing many favorite songs as we travel. Sometimes we try new ones. Singing is a good release for restless children. It refreshes all who join and adds spiritual dimension to the journey.

In a family of adolescent boys, the oldest had just passed his examination for a driver's license. He came home pleased and excited and full of details of the experience. The conversation during supper was the recounting of the events, the advice he received, the hazards to be avoided, what was lawful, and what was not lawful.

Father, appreciating the importance of the time, not only for the son but for all the family, suggested a family prayer for the one who, having just received his license to drive, was assuming responsibility of great importance to himself and countless others.

Two years later, the second son passed his examination for a driver's license. After supper he put his arm around his father's shoulder and asked, "How about a family prayer for me tonight, Dad? I think I need it as much as Arthur."

When the Fred Miller family built a new house they found ways to make such an undertaking of spiritual significance. Not only did they as a family seek God's guidance together before building, but when they moved in they planned a special service of dedication. They invited their pastor and family plus several close friends to share with them in dedicating their home to God, in promising to seek to keep their home the kind of place in which Christ feels welcome, and in which friends and strangers will find a refuge of love.

For Special Strength

When young people go away to school or service it is a great moment in family life. If our homes are to be spiritual launching platforms from which we send our children step by step to serve a world, then these moments of launching should carry a spiritual impact. The sharing of some guiding words from Scripture and the pause in prayer by the gathered family at such a time is an unforgettable experience.

A young man serving in one of the world's trouble spots was asked by a friend, "How is it possible for you

to stick it out in such a situation? Aren't the temptations terrific?" "Yes," he answered, "the temptations
are tremendous. But I can still hear my father and
mother's prayer when I was ready to leave home. They
prayed God to keep me from wrong and to help me to
be faithful to Him and to the teaching they sought to
give me. I know my family is praying fervently for me
as I serve here."

Marriage is a moment of spiritual significance. It
should be a joyous experience. Too often even Christian
young people can recall their wedding day only as a day
of frills, food, and foolish stunts. Here we as Christian
parents are challenged to add spiritual dimension. It is
not so much a time to preach to those getting married as
a time to teach younger children the meaning of marriage. It is a time for parents to share with children their
own love for each other and how God led them together.

"I remember when my cousin was married," said a
happily married young wife, "how my parents, on the
way home from the wedding, shared something of the
joy they experienced when they were married. When
they told us that their love for each other and their happiness now was greater than ever, I felt a sense of well-
being that has given me stability many times since. That
experience has cast a light across my entire life that I
feel I could not live without."

Even the death of a friend or of one in the family can
be a moment of a growing spiritual experience. Such an
experience can be the means of instilling confidence in
God far beyond and different from nearly any other experience. Here, in the time of separation and what
seems to be the end, the child can be taught by the
spirit, attitude, and words of parents, those things which
are eternal. Here, for the Christian, is the opportunity
to share deeply in the sorrow which is normal, but also

to show clearly that faith in God frees us from fatalism and hopelessness. Even in the fact of death a family's faith can flower forth.

In our family it was the practice to take all the children to the funeral of a relative or friend. The way in which my father and mother shed tears of sorrow and sympathy, the words of hope they spoke to the bereaved, and the Christian message preached on such occasions have helped much in giving to me a blessed and living hope.

The Andrew family took their two small sons to the funeral of a great-uncle the boys knew well. "We expected to be faced with many questions, and we were," said Mrs. Andrew. "But the fact that death represented no fear for them was what amazed me. Eight-year-old James talked calmly about death and seeing God. Four-year-old John wondered why he must wait to be older to die. We were happy to have assurance of life after death so that we could lead them in the conceptions of life, death, and heaven."

When We Worship and Witness

Family worship need not be a thing of the past. For years many received a God-consciousness around the family altar which today's family might well cherish.

"This morning I saw a beautiful picture," said a friend of mine as we met before a conference session. We were staying in different homes during a conference held in a college community.

Then he told me the scene he saw when he came down for breakfast. Seated around the table was the entire family, the college chemistry professor and wife and their five children. The children, ranging in age from five to later teens, had their Bibles and songbooks. After singing several songs they took turns reading the

Scripture and praying. This family started the day with spiritual strength.

Through family worship children learn their relation also to the larger family of God. As they pray in the family circle for the church, its ministers and its worldwide mission, their love and loyalty for Christ and the church grows. As children's interests and friendships broaden to include people outside the family and close friends, so family prayers broaden in scope as children become missionary-minded in the basic sense of having concern for all people.

Nursery-age Bobby, thinking of his father's house-to-house sales contacts, included his father's customers in his prayer when he asked God, "Please bless all the folks I don't know."

Many times I am amazed at the deep concern children have for others. After sharing someone's need, I have heard small children, on their own, remember that person in prayer day after day. So also in the hearing of daily news concerning physical and spiritual need, concerning war and peace, we have another opportunity to clothe such with spiritual meaning and purpose.

In Deuteronomy 6:6, 7 God tells us that the task of teaching and using available moments to teach is no hit-and-run method. "And these words which I command you this day shall be upon your heart; and you shall teach them diligently to your children, and shall talk of them when you sit in your house, and when you walk by the way, and when you lie down, and when you rise."

From one point of view it is "easy" to mold children. That is, children are impressionable. They are easily persuaded of the truth of what their parents teach them.

On the other hand, it is a tremendous undertaking to give children a genuine Christian nurture and training. It is much easier for parents to neglect than to nurture their children for God. This is the reason for the almost tedious emphasis of the Scripture that parents speak of God and His works under all circumstances. When sitting in one's house, when walking in the way, when retiring for the night, when arising, whether relaxed at home, or hurrying along a hot and dusty road, the conversation shall often turn to God and His Word.

To tell about God when retiring, arising, sitting, or walking does not, of course, mean incessant chattering about religion. It means only that our faith will be so meaningful to us that it will be natural in all circumstances of life to speak of God and His works. Notice that God says, "These words which I command you this day shall be upon your heart."

So it is that we, as parents, have precious opportunities to relate all life to God. But opportunities are passing things. Opportunities must be seized immediately or they are lost. We are called to make the most of every opportunity for God in the only family we will ever have. We are called to make our families demonstration centers of Christian living.

If, as Henry Drummond wrote, "The family circle is the supreme conductor of Christianity," then we must hallow the daily duties and delights of family living with the touch of the divine.

MAKING FAMILY
LIFE SPIRITUAL

1. List occasions and opportunities in your home which could be made more meaningful and spiritual in character.

2. How can we convey spiritual truth without becoming preachy to our children?

3. How can we keep worship and spiritual disciplines from becoming routine?

6

Courtesy—Caught and Taught

A hurt look was in Sandra's eyes. "Dad," she said, "sometimes I wish you were more polite." Shocked, I asked Sandra what she meant. She explained kindly, yet in very clear terms.

Sandra had come to show me her fourth-grade spelling test paper. Her smile showed the satisfaction she felt in making a good grade. And I, instead of seeing her paper and sharing in her achievement, looked up and said, "Sandra, your hair is hanging in your face. I can hardly see your eyes."

Now I sensed the hurt and apologized. I told Sandra I would try to do better. Although I did not mean to be rude, I saw that my concern about adult conventions made me callous to the courtesy my child deserved. Sandra, by her remark, stimulated me to do some serious thinking on courtesy.

Like any parent, I try to teach my children to be courteous. One of the first things I found true was that I told my children to be courteous more than I showed them courtesy. Of course, there must be precept as well as practice but, as with most things, courtesy is caught more than taught.

What Is Courtesy

One of the credentials of Christianity is, "Be courteous." The word comes from the manner of the court. It means to be kingly. Courtesy is that fine flower of life which carries a sweet fragrance wherever it goes. Courtesy is speech seasoned with love. It is action motivated by affection. It is based upon inner attitudes and reveals concern for the happiness and rights of others. Courtesy is the overflow and outflow of kindness and patience, and the desire for the other's best.

Of course, there is a superficial courtesy which is put on the outside. It may arise out of a desire for approval or popularity or reputation. Such may be illustrated by the man who takes off his manners with his hat when he enters his house or the wife who treats outsiders better than insiders.

One person describes courtesy like this: "Courtesy is showing love for other people in even our smallest actions. Whether or not to wear gloves on a particular social occasion is only a minor matter, you see. In the long run it probably doesn't matter much. But rushing ahead of another person, trampling over his feelings by the things we say, or laughing into his face are serious acts of discourtesy because they are actions which do not express love for the person. So, basic good manners spring from a heart of love for people." Courtesy is more than proper etiquette. It is not only "put on" manners. Christian courtesy is "put in" manners.

Breaches of Courtesy

As in the case with Sandra, we as parents may find that our practice of politeness is rather poor. We break the rules. We many times expect more courtesy of our children than we practice ourselves.

In *Homes Build Persons* the author writes, "We parents should realize, though we seldom do, that our children have about as much worry and anxiety over our manners and conduct as we have over theirs."

Because children are not adults we tend to ignore their questions and concerns. Children ask questions. They call for attention in many ways. These questions and calls can be used as occasions to build relationships and understandings. Yet many times, simply because we are discourteous, we miss the opportunity.

Adults have a bad habit of butting in when children are talking. One day while visiting in a home, the little man of the house and I were alone in the living room. He was explaining to me a most exciting thing he was doing. He was building a tepee under a tree in the backyard. He planned to sleep in it some night.

In the middle of his story his father stepped into the room and without excusing himself interrupted his small son and told me dinner was ready. I noticed the hurt look on the lad's face. His father did not mean to be discourteous. To me his words of invitation to dinner were gracious. But for some strange reason he felt no need to be courteous to his own son, since he was small. The boy showed better manners when he whispered to me as we went to the dining room, "Maybe after dinner I can tell you the rest, OK?"

It is a breach of courtesy when adults laugh at questions or remarks of a child. Just as serious is to repeat silly little mistakes children make to get a laugh when friends visit. Not only is it discourteous but it destroys trust and self-confidence in the child.

In his fine book, *A Parents' Guide to Emotional Needs of Children,* Dr. David Goodman writes: "To be courteously treated by parents makes a child feel sure of his own worth. That's important to his all-around sense of security and self-confidence. It is with his self-confidence that a child makes his way in the world. That is the great endowment we bestow upon our children. Without it all other gifts are worthless." And in a society of depersonalization courtesy can go a long way to meet the desperate need for recognition and acceptance.

Often parents, because they feel better qualified to answer questions, do not let the child answer for himself when spoken to. Think how discourteous this is by considering how it sounds when applied to the adult world.

Closely connected to the act of speaking for the child is the contradiction of what the child says. There is a way of kindly correcting without openly contradicting.

So also when parents rise from the table or leave the room when a child is talking, there is a breach of courtesy. Parents are sometimes rude in forcing a child to be polite. Ever hear a parent yell in anger to a child, "Don't interrupt me"? Further, there is little hope of helping a child to be courteous by telling him he is rude or impolite. The fact is that children have a way of living up to their reputation. The child who is merely told that he is impolite is hardly helped. He is just reminded of impoliteness and will likely live up to it again.

Where Courtesy Begins

Where, then, do we begin to teach our children courtesy? We begin at the place we begin in just about everything else, with ourselves. Since courtesy is caught more than taught, parents must look at their own relationships and practices. Courtesy is home-grown.

One minister in counseling persons before marriage has the practice of consistently asking one question of each partner. "John, I want you to promise me that you will at all times be as courteous to Mary as you are to other men's wives." Of course, John nods and says, "Yes, sir." He could not imagine at this stage anything else. Then he asks, "And Mary, will you promise me that you will, at all times, be as courteous to John as you are to other women's husbands?" Unhesitatingly, Mary answers, "Yes."

We expect courtesy to play a prominent part in courtship, but it is good to remember that manners affect marriage more than anything else. The wedding day dare not be the end of knighthood and the beginning of serfdom. For courtesy is not only a preparation for marriage but also a preservative of marriage.

Courtesy is a basic and a most important means of expressing love. One marriage counselor says, "Lack of courtesy on the part of husband or wife is the basic cause of 80 percent of the coldness and estrangements, if not absolute quarrels and separation, in married life."

A lack of courtesy also allows a coldness to develop between parents and child. And since courtesy is born in the atmosphere of the home, children in their relationship to others, in a large measure, reflect that atmosphere. A leisurely, gracious, serene, and happy atmosphere will do more than a dozen commands.

Sometimes we get the curious idea that we should be courteous to folks outside our family, but at home it doesn't matter. One mother was shocked when her small daughter said to her, "Mother, I wish you would be as nice to us as you are to other people." Suddenly she became aware that she did treat her family different from friends.

We build courtesy best when we are courteous to our children. I was in a home in which I sensed the children had a sense of propriety. I would take a lesson. The father, desiring a favor of his son, said, "John, would you please get me my checkbook from the study?" The mother in expressing appreciation said, "Jane, thank you for washing out the washbowl today. It looked so sparkly when I got home."

But not only did it work this way but I saw time and again that the parents were quick to help their children. Jane needed her book from the study. "Just a minute, Jane," her father said as he walked toward the room, "I'll bring it for you." And the mother noticing that Jane had numerous studies for the evening, said at supper, "Jane, I'll be glad to do the dishes myself, since I've caught up with my work. You'll need the time for study."

In this story are other secrets to build courtesy. It is a sublime act of courtesy to greet our children and others by name. "Good morning, John" imparts warmth and love, for it is still true there is no sound as sweet as our own name. A word of praise, rather than to nag or blame, will get one much further in the long run. Then too, small words open the heart. As an old nursery rhyme puts it:

> Hearts, like doors, will open with ease
> To very, very little keys,
> And don't forget that two of these
> Are "I thank you" and "if you please."

Courtesy Is Respect for Persons

Courtesy, at its best, is a spiritual quality born out of reverence and regard for the individual. Garry and Caroline Myers, in their book *Homes Build Persons,* say, "Let us remember that we do best at teaching good manners to the child as we prove by our self-discipline that we have great regard for him as a person and are, therefore, courteous to him." Someone said, "Jesus never met an unimportant person."

To be courteous is to respect the person as a person, one of God's creation. This means no exception—rich or poor, educated or uneducated. The way parents treat the mailman, milkman, and garbage collector; the way parents talk to the teller at the bank; and the way they speak to their neighbors build or destroy respect for persons. The kindness shown to all persons, regardless of who they are, provides the path to the practice of courtesy by our children.

I appreciate the story of President Abraham Lincoln who demonstrated his respect for persons at a state dinner in the White House.

An hour or so before dinner a party of his former country store friends dropped in to see him, naturally planning to stay for dinner. Lincoln ordered the table rearranged and seated the politicians and the backwoods friends together around the table.

During the meal one of his country friends poured coffee into his saucer, blew over it to cool it, and drank from the saucer.

Lincoln noticed his critics lifting eyebrows, exchanging glances, smiling. While they watched for his response, the president lifted his cup, poured coffee into the saucer, blew over it, and drank from his saucer. His critics were big enough to take the cue and that day around the White House table all the guests drank coffee from their saucers.

Perhaps parents teach more about respect for persons by what they say when people are absent than by the way they perform when present. The child whose family indulges in joking about personality traits and acts and lives of other persons—by this saying they are inferior and ridiculous—will have a hard time being courteous to these persons. One person, who as a small lad, visited in a home which seemed to delight in telling stories about others in order to get a laugh, says that although he was young he sensed the unkindness of this and knew it was wrong. He developed a distaste for visiting in that home.

We teach children to distrust others by the questions raised about their friends. To criticize a child's playmate is a most discourteous act. A little girl prayed, "God, help bad people to be good, and all good people to be nice."

In a questionnaire children were asked what they wished their parents would do and not do. Three things stood at the top: treat my friends like they are welcome and try to understand us; tell me right from wrong, but don't be too mean about it; don't fuss at me in front of other people.

I like Henry Drummond's definition of courtesy: "Love is little things." Someone suggests that the three miracle words in the family are "pardon me," "please," and "thank you." Love says "pardon me" because it recognizes the dignity of the other. Love says "please" because it acknowledges the kindness of the other person. Love says "thank you" because it feels and expresses gratitude for the other person. Love must find expression in words such as these or it loses its luster and beauty.

Courtesy is a part of character and skill. As such, teaching is also important. One writer put it this way: "Suppose that all your life you would observe good eating habits at the table; you always chew with your lips closed. I don't think that example is going to get the idea across to the children. I think that in addition to closing your mouth when you chew, you are going to have to tell the children to do that. You might spend your whole lifetime being careful not to look into another person's pocketbook or mail. But I don't believe that fact is going to teach your children not to look into someone else's pocketbook. You will need to tell them."

So it is true that the promptings of parents are needed in addition to proper example. Good manners are learned also like any good character trait "here a little, and there a little . . . line upon line . . . precept . . . upon precept." Children need to be taught respect for the possessions and rights of others. Father has his desk; Mother has her dresser. Letters are private things, and it is the right thing to knock before entering the bathroom or the room of another person.

In our family we had what we called the good manners club. If one member caught another who forgot to say "please" or "thank you," or who interrupted a conversation, or walked in front of another without a "pardon me," he became president of the club. He remained president until he was caught not minding his manners. As you can imagine, parents were caught as often as children. Perhaps it is not healthy to keep such a club going for a long stretch of time. It is one method, however, of cultivating a conscience on courtesy.

Finally, it's just about as simple as deciding what we want. We must choose to be courteous and develop the discipline of courtesy each day. We do not stumble into being a gentleman or lady. The home that has no time for courtesy will have time for rudeness. The home that does not take time for compliments will have time for complaints. The home that has no time for smiles will have time for frowns. And the home that has no time for sweet loving words will find time for harsh, critical words.

An unknown author wrote:

> I am a little thing with a big meaning.
> I help everyone.

I unlock doors, open hearts, banish prejudice:
I create friendship and goodwill.
I inspire respect and admiration.
I violate no law.
I cost nothing.
Many have praised me; none have condemned me.
I am pleasing to those of high and low degree.
I am useful every moment.
I am courtesy.

COURTESY — CAUGHT AND TAUGHT

1. Write a definition of courtesy.

2. List breaches of courtesy in addition to those listed in the article.

3. How many parents in the group consistently say "thank you," "please," and "pardon me" in the home? Why is our practice at home different from that away from home?

7

Winning the Chore War

WHAT can we do to get our children to help around the house?" This question, asked in a parents' study group by one frustrated mother, sounds familiar to many families. It points to a perennial problem of parents. What can parents do to train children to help in the home?

Of course, we should not believe the myth that parents can be so skillful in setting the family stage that each child will always naturally want to peel potatoes, scrub floors, make beds, sweep and dust, wash dishes, and willingly do all that should be done. But parents can be assured that there are principles all parents can follow to develop in children a healthy attitude toward work.

Begin Early

Welcome warmly the child's first efforts to help. The parent who compliments the child's earliest cooperation in such things as putting his arm into his sleeve, washing his hands, or eating by himself cultivates a helpful attitude.

A child loves to help. So much so that at times he can become an annoyance. As one mother of two small children commented, "They help me from morning until night and I get things done in twice the time it would take me to do it alone." Yes, it is much quicker for parents to do small chores themselves. A schoolteacher can also add and spell better and faster than her pupils.

But she knows how important it is to give the child a chance to learn. So also does the wise parent.

One morning two-year-old Sandra was suspiciously quiet in the bathroom. When her mother looked in, she saw Sandra had smeared toothpaste over mirror, washbowl, walls, and floor. Like any parent, her first inclination was to punish, to make it plain to Sandra that such behavior is bad. But Sandra may have had good intentions. Perhaps she was trying to clean like she saw her mother clean. Besides, squeezing the toothpaste was fun. The soft, smooth feel in spreading it around no doubt gave her a pleasant and satisfying sensation.

Sandra's mother recognized her interest in helping and took the first step in teaching her how to clean the mirror and wash the bowl properly. Sure it is simpler to scold or spank in such a situation. But it is better to take time to give guidance. A little time at two can save much time and tension at twelve.

Even the toddler can be helpful. He can be taught to join in the fun of picking up toys and putting them in the proper place. In *The Strategy of Handling Children,* D. A. Laird says that children should be "started in the habit of keeping things picked up as soon as they are big enough to crawl around. Nine out of ten children can be given the habit of orderliness from their toddler days."

To begin early does not mean to saddle the child with numerous responsibilities. While a child with nothing to do becomes bored, a child with too much to do becomes frustrated. The important thing is for each child to have some regular responsibility. Additional work can be given gradually and increased as the child grows older.

In assigning work, keep in mind that a child at various age levels has different attention spans. Give short jobs to the younger, and chores taking more time to the more mature.

Remember, one secret in securing a child's help in the home is to start early taking time to teach when the child wants to help.

Dampening the early and deep desires a child has to help is sometimes the start of the later problem of the child not wanting to help. To respect the initial exuberance of childhood expressed in the spirit of "let me help" or "I'm helping too" is a good start in helping the child assume responsibility.

Encourage Initiative

One step beyond honoring the child's first desire to help is to seek to stimulate the child to try many different things.

Often the child is stimulated when parents simply allow the child to share in small things. He is encouraged to be helpful when allowed to carry small packages on the family shopping trip. He is stimulated to hang up his clothes when parents place hanging rods low enough for him to reach. He is spurred on to wash his hands if a box-step puts the washbowl within easy reach.

Initiative is also stimulated by permitting some leeway to do things, to investigate, and to try new projects.

Take the time ten-year-old Billy started a thriving shoe-shining business. He made his own awkward-looking but functional shoe kit. The family discussed what a fair charge might be for various kinds of footwear. For a time Billy earned extra money keeping all the family's shoes polished to a high gloss. True, the project was of short duration, but his parents encouraged him and made allowance for the natural ups and downs of enthusiasm.

A child is a great fixer. He loves to experiment, to see how things are made, and how they work. To develop initiative, capitalize on this love by letting the child try his hand at fixing things.

Permitting the child to join in planning and preparing for something he likes to do encourages initiative. The Williams' children, like most children, are sociable. They enjoy parties and guests. But this involves extra work. When the children asked for a party, the entire family took time to sit down to discuss what it means to have friends come. During the discussion each decided on something to do to lighten the load for Mother. What was often drudgery became delight. Now cleaning, washing dishes, and helping to make the meal had meaning. Further, each child had an inner joy because he was making a particular contribution.

A child wants to do what he sees adults do. Right here initiative can be stifled or stimulated. It takes fortitude and faith to stand back and let a child assume the responsibility he reaches out for. But what if eggs do break? Better broken eggs than a broken spirit. What if a cake burns or milk is spilled? Better this than discouraging a child to help. If he overreaches a little, never mind. Just help him to grow up to it. It takes a sense of timing to keep responsibility fitted to the growing, and to recognize and respect a child's abilities and limitations. True, parents sometimes push too much responsibility on a child. But it is perhaps more prevalent and just as wrong to push the child away by continually saying things like "Not now. Wait until you are bigger."

Express Appreciation

Appreciation is the key which unlocks a helpful spirit in the home. Parents are prone to think a child's work their due. It is easier to correct and criticize than to commend. If parents desire to teach their child to work, they must accept the challenge to celebrate the child's successes. Jane Grossman writes in *Life with Family* that "celebrating success is important. We should register our pleasure and satisfaction when a son or daughter shows improvement in a heretofore difficult course, when work is well done."

The child receives encouragement to help in the home from these first expressions of appreciation. A smile when the child first picks something up from the floor stimulates the spirit of helpfulness. A generous use of compliments calls out the best. And parents who practice praising their child for work well done will find him living up to his reputation. They will also find him more ready to respond rightly in other areas of living.

In his book *How to Help Your Child Grow Up*, Angelo Patri says that just as every artist needs an audience and perishes without one, so every child who does something of achievement needs to be praised. The young performer is inspired by the acceptance and approval of his elders whom he longs to please.

Perhaps it seems inconsequential to say to a young son, "That was a good job you did," when he fixes a doorknob or puts a new washer in the faucet. But it isn't. It may seem insignificant for Mother to tell her teenage daughter, "I feel safe when you are taking care of your brother." But such statements call forth an attitude of even greater responsibility. When Father asks, "Mother, did you see Danny help me clean the garage today?" he is instilling in Danny the thrill of achievement and the joy of joining another in some work.

Parents who regularly express appreciation to their child will find it returned in many ways, including help in household work.

But what is the proper kind of praise? Praise should be specific. To express appreciation to Johnny for helping his baby sister put on her rubbers is much better than blanket praise such as, "Johnny, you were a good boy today." Perhaps Johnny is reminded, with such a blanket compliment, of something he did which was not good. To thank six-year-old Ann for helping Mother set the table or clean the playroom has far deeper meaning than to say simply, "Thank you for helping Mother so well today."

Praise a child for doing things which required effort, self-sacrifice, or a right response. To praise a child for such things as blue eyes or beautiful clothes, which do not come by personal effort, can be harmful rather than helpful.

Praise should not create the impression that the child is working for external rewards. There should be no idea that parents owe money or special favors because a child helps a bit around the house. Home is a cooperative effort, not a commercial enterprise. Allowances should bear no relation to obligations and responsibilities as members of the family. While it may be valid to pay for extra-special work occasionally, this should not lead the child to expect pay for daily duties. Sincere words of appreciation for work well done is the pay most children miss yet need most.

Be Companions

"The more agreeable and companionable the child's relationships with his parents, the more willing he is to share in household duties and drudgeries," says one authority. "It is hard to duplicate the closeness and sense of sharing when parents and children work side by side."

Jeff Andrews typifies the approach of a parent working with his children. One evening he was telling his neighbor about the big job coming up next day. He needed to trim some trees and landscape a large part of the lawn. After discussing the work, he turned to his two boys standing by his side and said, "We can get it all done in one day, can't we, boys?" They responded with readiness.

Tim had a small garden. The weeds were getting ahead and he was rather discouraged. One evening Mr. Andrews said, "Tim, tomorrow is Saturday. Suppose I go along with you out to your garden and help get rid of the weeds. An hour should do it." Next morning Tim was up early and ready to go to work. Not only was Tim's father helping him, but his father was also his companion in work.

Many a mother has learned that washing dishes can be a delight for mother and daughter if they do them together. And many a father knows that his son responds much more readily when he asks his son to help him with a task rather than demanding the son do it himself.

Of course, jobs cannot always be done together. However, an overall feeling of togetherness can be developed. In *Bringing Up Children* Langdon and Stout write, "It is a good idea to think of a child's responsibilities as just part of everyday family living, not merely the doing of certain assigned chores. . . . They come to a child because he is one involved in all the family affairs. They are a natural part of living."

When the family finds projects in which all share, there are added opportunities for learning to help. The Fishers moved into an old house. In spite of age, however, the house was solid and still showed that at one time it was beautiful and even luxurious. Now it needed a family to own it and to lavish love and care upon it.

All this meant countless real work projects. Many trees and rosebushes needed to be cut and trimmed. There were all kinds of jobs for parents and children.

Before the house was bought the involvements were discussed in the family council and the work laid out.

Now they scrubbed and painted, trimmed and mowed, landscaped and planted, until it was restored to something of its old atmosphere and beauty. They also rescued, repaired, and refinished old furniture. Their home was not only a training place for developing work habits, but an opportunity in building togetherness.

"A very young child, especially if his efforts are appreciated, will form ties with the places where he has accomplished something worthwhile that will always remain sources of satisfaction," says Lillian M. Gilbreth in *Living with Our Children.*

And it is those things which families do together which linger longest in the memory.

Be Consistent

Consistency must characterize the parents who desire their child to see the value of work and to help in the home. There should first be consistency in requiring a job to be done. The real joy and feeling of responsibility for a task dwindles when it is required one day, ignored the next, then demanded again. It is far better to have one job done well each day than to have a half dozen done poorly and with frequent reminders. A child, to have effective work habits, must learn to form such habits in the routine of everyday homelife.

If work is left undone, there should be consistency also in carrying out a penalty. It is good that the child knows the penalty beforehand. Never should work be assigned as a penalty. This helps form wrong attitudes toward work. Rather, withhold some pleasure and enforce it without fail.

Although each child should have a definite and regular responsibility, consistency does not mean a child should forever do the same job. What parent has not heard the argument of favoritism about the division of work? One way to avoid arguments is to rotate chores: Alice washes dishes one week, Judy washes them the next, and so on. Children like variation and this can develop broader skills and interests.

One mother suggests that a list of the chores be made, using a separate slip of paper for each job. Then mix them and let each child draw a slip to learn what his job will be for the day or week.

A child also has a keen sense of fairness. That sense is best satisfied when parents are considerate and consistent both in the requests and requirements of homelife.

Maintain Right Attitudes

Parents' attitudes toward work deeply influence the child's attitude. A child usually respects work when his parents look upon their work with respect and dignity, as well as with satisfaction. Such expressions as "I don't want my child to work, sacrifice, and struggle like I had to as a child" can cause only harm. Foolish, childish charges of lack of love like "After all I do for you, you ought to do some things for me," can only have an adverse effect.

Two boys, who today are a tribute to their parents, stood by the side of their father one day when he said to a friend, "I am glad for my work. In fact, I think one of the worst things that can happen to a healthy person is to be out of a job." Some time ago one of these young men said, "You know, in our home we never had much fuss about doing jobs around the place. Today, as I look back, I believe my parents' attitude toward work is what made work enjoyable for us."

In the home is found the earliest inspiration for work. The home is the basic working unit—father, mother, and children. Work is necessary. It must be learned.

And work can be fun. Success and achievement are delightful. There is added warmth when all share in the bright glow of one another's achievements and triumphs.

So swift are the years when we and our children grow older together. How soon the time of sharing in work and play passes. It is good to know that all are needed to make a contribution, large or small, for the sake of one another and ourselves. It is this realization that Kahlil Gibran's words have meaning, "Work is love made visible."

To the parents who ask, "Can we do anything to get our children to help in the home?" the answer is, "Yes." At any point parents can begin to teach wholesome attitudes toward toil which make helping interesting and natural.

WINNING THE CHORE WAR

1. Discuss first if this is a problem in your home.

2. What seems to get the best response from your children?

3. Probably the area of most failures is that parents do not express enough appreciation to their children. Is this true?

4. What are the things the modern family could do together or share in?

8

Parents Teach Sex

"MY parents never told me anything about sex. When I got married I knew next to nothing about what the sex act involved. When my husband tried to help me understand I felt guilty for a long time. Even now as a mother of grown children I sometimes feel bitter and get emotionally upset because I feel my parents failed me in this." This experience from one mother is not unusual.

A common complaint of youth is expressed by a ninth-grade boy. "I wouldn't trust myself to ask my parents about sex. If I slipped and used a dirty word, they'd drop dead from shock."

A freshman girl confided in her college counselor, "I could never ask my mother any questions about sex because right away she fired back, 'What do you want to know for?'"

Many parents find sex education a real problem. Some feel uncomfortable about the public schools teaching sex because they know sex is more than mere facts. There is a spiritual and sacred side which the schools can hardly be expected to teach. Values need to be taught. Yet, knowing that sex education is necessary and that the responsibility falls primarily on parents, many continue to feel incompetent because they think they know too little, guilty because they think they say too little, and fearful lest they use a wrong approach.

Sex is a difficult subject for anyone to discuss. You may shudder to think of the time when your child will come with the first question about birth or reproduction. You may feel you failed when you had opportunity to teach or may be secretive about the subject of sex because of hang-ups you experience. You do not feel free to share.

"At the same time," says Millard J. Bienvenu, Sr., head of the Department of Sociology at Northwestern State College of Louisiana and author of *Parent-Teenager Communication,* "we have come to realize that the best way to help children grow up with a healthy and decent appreciation of sex is to avoid being secretive about it. Today's youth have available to them more information and mis-information and are exposed to more sexual stimuli than ever before. Consequently it is imperative that they get the information which will shape their attitudes first from the parents."

Actually the experience of homes for unmarried mothers and courts for delinquents teaches that the majority of young people who get into trouble have had very little factual information about sex.

Two preliminary points are important as a start on the subject of sex.

All Parents Are Teaching Sex

First, whether we know it or not, we, as parents, are teaching sex. We cannot avoid it. Every moment, by the way we live, by our attitudes, by what we say or do not say, we are teaching that which has very much to do with our child's understanding and approach to sex.

Early the child senses love and acceptance. He can interpret the tone of voice and the touch of the hand. But most of all his understanding of sex stems from what he senses in the relationships between his mother and father.

Sex too often is limited to a discussion of sexual intercourse. It is much more. It includes free com-

munication, acts of love and kindness, and a relationship in which parents enjoy each other. When mother
and father love each other and are not hesitant to show
it and say it, children do not need to be told that sex is
beautiful. They see it, feel it, and know it. When there is
tension between mother and father, no amount of talking about the beauty or sanctity of sex will get the message across.

Parents' own marital relationships and attitudes toward sex are the first things to look at in working toward a better understanding of sex on the part of children. Further, parents must be able to communicate
freely between themselves before sharing with the child
can be as successful as it should be. So the child's con-
cept of sex comes by observing and sensing the closeness of parents and by enjoyable physical contacts beginning in infancy—the loving kiss and hug and the oc-
casional pat on the shoulder. The child's approach to
sex is also learned from the reaction of parents to statements about sex. By all of these means parents are always, each moment, teaching something about sex.

Facts Should Be Shared Early

A second important point is that sex facts such as the
difference between male and female, the body functions,
and changes, as well as reproduction, ought to be
shared as fully as possible before such facts carry emotional freight. This means that parents ought to present
such facts before children reach adolescence when
young people have enough other problems to trouble
them in the turbulent teens. Psychiatrist Paul Conrad
says, "The ages one through five are the most significant
years in sex education. Sex information should be im-
parted before the age of six." Why should some parts of
the body be referred to in mysterious and meaningless

terms? We do not learn foreign names for our fingers and feet.

If the facts of sex, which are really few, are shared before the child reaches eleven or twelve, he comes to the teen years with an understanding and a freedom he deserves. This knowledge also gives him a real sense of security and strength.

If a girl knows about such things as menstruation and other changes she will experience before they actually take place, she is prepared and accepts such changes as normal. She is then relaxed and happy in these changes. She lives in confidence. An understanding of the sex act relieves the child of ignorance and curiosity. "It is curiosity and ignorance," according to one experienced counselor, "which gets most girls into trouble."

When a boy is told about such things as wet dreams, circumcision, and reproduction by a loving parent before adolescence when such subjects become highly emotional, he is well on the way to making correct and mature adjustments. His mind is also more at ease. And he is more likely to come to his parents for additional help later on.

Many questions young people ask reveal that misinformation and rumor are still the rule rather than the exception. If parents share facts early enough much mental and emotional strain, as well as misinformation, will be avoided. Much inquisitive exploration, which usually produces guilt feelings, can be eliminated. Further, the child with factual information comes with confident understanding to those situations in which young people share sex stories which are incorrect, confusing, and carry lifelong but wrong impressions.

In addition to these two overall guides certain simple specific suggestions are helpful.

Be Biblical

Begin with the basic biblical facts. We warp and twist life when we try to ignore something God has put within us and expects of us. God made us male and female. These are inescapable facts. And God made us this way for a purpose and proclaims His creation very good.

A big part of the problem in religious circles is that the moralizing about sex is mostly negative. A few generations ago some thought the admission of the sex urge was wrong. A hush-hush attitude prevailed. The Christian attitude is that sex is neither to be ashamed of or something to be exploited. It is a normal and wholesome part of life, as normal and wholesome as any other.

So the Bible begins with the fact of sexuality. God made male and female. Maleness and femaleness are essentials of our humanity. There is no shame in God's work. Passionate affection was present before the Fall. The Fall of man did not create sex or passion. It perverted it. The libertine and the prude are equally under the judgment of God in their lack of biblical understanding of sexuality.

As David A. Hubbard writes: "What's wrong with the *Playboy* philosophy? It's not that Hugh Hefner talks too much about sex; he doesn't talk enough. It's not that sex is made too important in *Playboy* magazine and other organs of the mass media; it is not important enough. An English writer, invited to go to the Playboy Club of London, declined. 'No, I don't want to go look at those bunnies. I'm too interested in sex,' a profound theological statement."

Sex is wholesome. We must start here if we are to educate properly. The Scripture does not avoid speaking frankly about sex. The fact is that the Scripture has some of the most forthright statements in all of literature. It is God who created us as intellectual, emotional, spiritual, social, and sexual beings.

Be Loving

Some see sex education as merely an explanation of biology, physiology, and anatomy, or they see it as a chance to inform teenagers about family planning or the danger of social diseases. This is inadequate. Many persons know all these facts and plenty of technique, yet never know the real meaning of sexuality because love is lacking. Such can know all the mechanics of mattress gymnastics, yet know little or nothing of what is involved for sex to have real meaning and enjoyment. Thus the experience itself is empty of inner satisfaction and the search goes on in illicit desires and acts. No amount of sex facts can ever make up for a lack of love.

To help persons understand themselves as persons and to appreciate the dignity of human love is the basic purpose of sex education. And the only way we learn to love is to be loved and to love in return. This is the reason for the family. Parents should daily display affection for each other within the family circle.

In a recent study of personality differences between girls who are virgins before marriage and those who are not shows that harshness of punishments and lack of love in the home was much more characteristic of those who had premarital sex relations. It is a loveless home which teaches youth that sex is the goal of living.

Sexuality at its best is freedom, tenderness, abandonment, love, and joy. And only parents can teach tenderness, freedom, and abandonment which comes in the presence of trust, protection, and love. So by the loving kiss, caress, and word even the small child learns his first lesson in what love is. Later he learns that sex belongs to the whole picture of love, caring, and sharing.

One young man tells how his attitudes regarding sex were formed when he saw the love his father had for his mother and sisters. "Often early in the morning my father would go out to find the most beautiful rosebud in the garden. He would place it at Mother's place to greet her when she came to breakfast. It cost only a few minutes of time and a heart full of love. But when he stepped behind her chair and she picked up the rose, and he gave her his morning kiss, the whole day was glorified. Even the child who had gotten out of bed on 'the wrong side,' felt ashamed because life had been touched by love. Now I think I understand why I always feel repulsed by those who consider a woman a cheap plaything. My parents illustrated to me what love and personhood really mean."

Be Natural

When a child asks questions about his sexuality he indicates a basic curiosity of life which is devoid of the emotional content which adults attach. Therefore, answer the child in a natural way. Parents dare never imply by attitude, word, or silence that sex is bad, distasteful, or less than beautiful and good.

Why, when a child asks a question in this area of life, do parents lower their voice, blush, remain silent, act shocked, ask the child why he wants to know, or start on a long lecture on reproduction? By these actions the child senses this area of life is somehow not normal and begins to build up barriers to understanding and appreciation. "Hush-hush" attitudes degrade sex. Welcome the child's questions and make him feel he was right in asking it of his parents.

Speak casually about love and affection, about pregnancy and childbirth in front of children. This produces the atmosphere conducive to easy questioning on the part of the child.

Because of certain circumstances or fears a child may not ask direct questions such as, "Where do babies come from?" However, he may ask all kinds of other questions, only tangential to sex, to the point that it may even be annoying. Parents should in these cases watch for a lead and use it to explain facts the children should know. Often a child suspects certain things, yet fears it is taboo to ask about it and so avoids the real question by asking all around it. However, he will never be satisfied until *the answer* is given. As we say "a question-box child" should be given "the answer" to the question he isn't asking.

Be Honest

Always answer a child's question honestly, directly, and accurately. Provide information suitable to the child's age and the question asked. A good guide to keep in mind is that expressed by Dr. H. Clair Amstutz in his excellent book, *Growing Up to Love:* "When a child is old enough to ask a specific question he has already proved himself capable of understanding a direct answer." If a parent is dishonest in explaining where children come from, why should the child not question the honesty of the parents about the evil of illicit sex later?

Vivian Ziegler, in a fine article entitled *Parents Are Sex Educators, Whether They Know It or Not,* writes, "The true story of reproduction is so marvelous that it is really puzzling why so many 'good' parents hope to improve on it by substituting the stork or the doctor's bag fables. Learning the correct terms for body parts and body functions at the beginning is a lot easier and better than discovering later."

So also explaining four-letter words which children

hear in the group or see scribbled on toilet walls takes away secretive meanings which cause fascination until explained. Remember to use proper terms and explain the unfamiliar ones to the child. Real words are not any more difficult to explain than difficult ones.

Be Alert

Teaching is a day-by-day process which proceeds from the known to the newly discovered. Parents can provide sex education by using the natural opportunities which come if they are alert to them. And such opportunities to impart knowledge come gradually and repeatedly. Not all needs to be told at once. Earlier discussions can always be returned to in order to add new information and emphasis.

A mother doesn't teach her daughter all about the art of cooking in one brief half-hour session. Neither does a father teach his son a trade in one formal session.

When the child comes with the first question, be glad and share joyfully and in a direct way. The child's coming shows a confidence the parent dare not lose. "Where did I come from, Mother?" "You grew in your mother's body. I carried you close to my heart." Such an answer with an affectionate hug teaches much. As time goes on more facts can be shared.

One of the best early opportunities for teaching is at the time the child receives a bath. It is not long until the child learns the name of his ear, eye, nose, fingers, and so on. One can also teach the child right terms for other parts of the body by talking while the bath is in progress. This way every part of the body can be referred to in a natural way.

Sometimes parents are slow to use such opportunities to share sexual information because they have the mistaken idea that the child feels and thinks the same as they. It is altogether natural for small children to be inquisitive about their own bodies and the bodies of others. This is no doubt God's way of assisting parents in their teaching. If parents are alert to this and satisfy their curiosity it will not need to be satisfied later. Wholesome information removes fear and erases unhealthy curiosity.

So as the child grows he is open to all kinds of things which can and will influence attitudes on sexuality. As the child grows the parents' primary job is to prepare the child to evaluate the influences rather than to shield him from them. It is more a matter of guidance than protection. And don't assume your child is different from others in what he knows. He likely knows a great deal more than you did at his age because he is bombarded by sex in so many ways today.

Be alert also, as a parent, to good reading material for yourself and for your child. Before the child can read himself, parents should read to him some of the excellent books available today on sex, which are written in a wholesome way. There is probably no more wonderful way to learn about where babies come from than to sit on the lap of mother or father, in the warmth of loving arms, and hear it from his own parents during times of relaxed reading. This also provides a better atmosphere for answering than the situation when the child pops the question, "Where do babies come from?" in the living room full of guests.

At appropriate times it will pay off to put the proper book or pamphlet in your child's room. There are numerous good books which can be given to your child which answer all the questions a young person at different age levels is likely asking, if not out loud, at least in the secrets of the heart.

Do not sneak a book into the child's room. Rather,

be open and honest enough to tell your child you think it is a good book and encourage him to read it.

Although it is not always possible, a good help in understanding of sex can be given when pets are kept around the house, particularly such pets as female dogs, cats, or tropical fish.

Be Happy

This means that parents should enjoy their respective roles if they are to teach the true meaning of sexuality. One author writes, "Many a woman dislikes or fears sex or is emotionally incapable of enjoying it because she has never learned deep in her unconscious mind to 'enjoy being a girl.' " A mother needs to glory in the fact that she is a woman and mother.

A mother who complains of her role, the drudgery of housework, the nuisance of children, the misery of menstruation, the pains of pregnancy and childbirth is teaching a lot about sex and is helping her son or daughter to maladjustment.

One happy wife writes, "When I saw the satisfaction my mother had in making a home, caring for a baby, and the way she enjoyed doing the things every woman needs to do, I felt the greatest thing in the world was to be a wife and mother. When I sensed her attitude of love and freedom toward my father, I felt the greatness of what it means to be a girl and woman and the goodness of relating to a man one loves. Also, as I saw my father's love and headship in the home, I decided what I desired in the one whom I would someday marry."

Of course, the same is true on the part of the father. Father sets the model of manhood before the children. For sons he provides something to measure up to, to identify with, to appreciate, and to admire. This does not mean father must be an athlete, a scholar, or the most handsome man in the block. It does mean that he must express himself in things specifically masculine.

One happy young husband writes: "No one showed me more of what it means to be a man and what it means to respect and love a woman than my own father. If he lacked many of the things some would call greatness, he was great in that he enjoyed being a man in his work, pastime activities, and as a father and husband in the home. His example is a challenge to me when my own family relationships seem frail."

In the words of Vivian Ziegler, in the article referred to earlier, "The reassuring fact is that if you as a parent accept your own sexuality and find joy in using it as a method of expressing love to your mate, you have very actively been giving sex education to your children since their birth in a positive, spontaneous, healthful, and God-intended way."

"It cannot be said too often," writes another authority, "that sex education is not the mastering of a set of do's and don'ts but the development of characteristics that produce loving and responsible persons."

PARENTS TEACH SEX

1. What do you think is the greatest problem you face in teaching sex to your children?

2. Is it true that "parents have little to fear from public school sex education if they have taught their children the basic facts and values of sex"?

3. What can be done to teach sex to teenagers if parents feel they have failed to teach the facts previous to the adolescent period?

4. What is your opinion of the statement by one psychiatrist that "the child should be taught the correct names of the sex organs, as well as the fingers, toes, and other parts of the body by the age three years"?

For Additional Reading and Reference

Alderfer, Helen and Edwin, *Help Your Child to Grow.* Herald Press.

Amstutz, H. Clair, *Growing Up to Love.* Herald Press.

Arnold, Eberhard, *Love and Marriage in the Spirit.* Plough.

Bienvenu, Millard J., Sr., *Parent-Teenager Communication. Public Affairs Pamphlet No. 438.*

Burns, Robert W., *The Art of Staying Happily Married.* Prentice-Hall, Inc.

Drescher, John M., *Meditations for the Newly Married.* Herald Press.

Duvall, Evelyn Milles, *Building Your Marriage.* Public Affairs Pamphlet No. 113, N.Y.

Erb, Alta, *Christian Nurture of Children.* Herald Press.

Faith at Work, "Marriage Is for Living." Zondervan.

Ginott, Haim G., *Between Parent and Child.* Macmillan.

Goodman, David, *A Parents' Guide to the Emotional Needs of Children.* Hawthorn.

Harrell, Irene, *Good Marriages Grow.* Word.

Hastings, Donald W., *A Doctor Speaks on Sexual Expression in Marriage.* Little, Brown.

Kennel, Lois and Arthur, MD., *Your Body and You.* Herald Press.

Mace, David R., *Success in Marriage.* Abingdon.

Myers and Myers, *Homes Build Persons.* Dorrance.

Shedd, Charlie W., *Letters to Karen: On Keeping Love in Marriage.* Abingdon.

Shedd, Charlie W., *Letters to Philip: Or How to Treat a Woman.* Doubleday.

Small, Dwight H., *After You've Said I Do.* Revell.

Small, Dwight H., *Design for Christian Marriage.* Revell.

Steinmetz, Urban G., *I Will*. Ave Maria Press and Pilgrim Press.

Tournier, Paul, *To Understand Each Other*. John Knox Press.

Webb, Lance, *Discovering Love*. Abingdon.

Winters, Gibson, *Love and Conflict*. Doubleday.

Ziegler, Vivian, *Parents Are Sex Educators, Whether They Know It or Not*. Messenger, Elgin, Ill.

A HANDBOOK FOR LIVING... WITH JOY!

In simple and straightforward language, Reverend John M. Drescher reveals the factors that bind a family together: the role of affection . . . how loving feelings are shared . . . how common courtesy can be the most valuable gift. Not least, he discusses the role that correct sex education plays in the teaching of love that enriches and lasts.

A noted writer on family problems and himself the father of five, the author sets forth guiding principles for every parent who seeks a successful Christian family life and desires his children's future happiness.